D1062775

SOULS
AT STAKE

by

REVEREND FRANCIS J. RIPLEY

AND

F. S. MITCHELL

WITH A FOREWORD BY THE

MOST REVEREND JOSEPH E. RITTER, S.T.D.
Archbishop of St. Louis

HOLY GHOST FATHERS
HOLY GHOST FATHERS
MISSION LIBRARY
48
NORWALK, CONN.

NEW YORK CITY

JOSEPH F. WAGNER, Inc.

LONDON: B. HERDER

BX809
C2
R5

J54
R

Nihil Obstat:

JOHN M. A. FEARNS, S.T.D.
Censor Librorum

Imprimatur:

✠ FRANCIS CARDINAL SPELLMAN, D.D.
Archbishop of New York

COPYRIGHT, 1948, BY JOSEPH F. WAGNER, INC., NEW YORK CITY

PRINTED IN THE UNITED STATES OF AMERICA

12941

FOREWORD

"Souls at Stake" is a book on the principles and technique of Catholic Action. In thirteen chapters it portrays techniques tried and true during the quarter-century in which the Legion of Mary has circled the globe. To name the Legion of Mary, however, is perhaps to limit the circulation of this excellent book. Let not the superlatives of encomium that have been heaped upon this providential lay movement prejudice the reader unacquainted with Mary's Army.

The co-authors—one a layman writing under the *nom de plume* of F. S. Mitchell and lending essays that appeared originally in *Maria Legionis*, the other Father Francis J. Ripley, priest of the Archdiocese of Liverpool—have given us in these essays the theology of the lay apostolate. The principles set forth are applicable to the lay apostolate, whether we find it operating under an official mandate of the Bishop (and hence entitled to the papal name, "Catholic Action"), or whether we find it simply under episcopal approbation and consequently designated by the more lowly title, "an auxiliary of Catholic Action."

The opening chapter graphically steers the thoughtful reader through the snares laid by the

iii

SEP 25 1981

Evil One to nullify the apostolate of the laity. (Our Catholic Faith cannot ignore the presence of the Prince of Darkness in the work of saving souls.) Action, prayer and perfect coöperation with priest and bishop are given their proper perspective, while the reader is safeguarded against the paralyzing emphasis on qualities desirable in the lay apostle, but seldom found in everyday life. The sound pedagogical principle of learning by doing is laid down as a foundation for effective apostolic work.

Modern secularism, so recently condemned by the American Hierarchy, is pictured in its effects on men of our age in such a way as to make imperative the counterattack of men and women of faith. But let the reader peruse this little volume himself for soul-stirring meditations on the infinite value of each individual soul, on radiating Christ, on Marriage as a vocation, on the rôle of the Christian educator, etc. Not the least among the essays, in our estimation, is that on *Social Action and the Catholic Apostolate* in its placing of first things first. To bolster his argument the author might have quoted, with his other excellent citations from Papal documents, the advice of Pius XI in his Encyclical on "Atheistic Communism," namely, that the primary remedy against this embodiment of all heresies is the teaching and living of the mysteries of the Redemption.

Some repetition may be expected in a compilation

such as "Souls at Stake." Far from being tedious, these repetitions are a delightful emphasis on a theme dear to every Bishop since he exhorts *all* candidates for Confirmation to be true "soldiers of Christ."

A fitting climax is reached in the concluding chapter on true devotion to Mary as essential to the lay apostolate. The sound theology lately canonized by our present Holy Father in raising St. Louis Marie de Montfort to our altars gives the devotional outlook for effective "lay participation in the work of the Hierarchy." All in all, "Souls at Stake" can be recommended as a companion volume to that gem of spiritual literature, "The Handbook of the Legion of Mary." Principles set forth in the one and in the other, when carried out by our zealous priests and devoted laity, will wring from priestly hearts the encomium we heard recently from a successful parish priest: "Of all that I have been privileged to do for this parish, my greatest contribution I judge to be my decision to inaugurate a Præsidium of the Legion of Mary."

MOST REVEREND JOSEPH E. RITTER,
Archbishop of Saint Louis.

Feast of Saint Francis Xavier, 1947

INTRODUCTION

IN THE CHRISTMAS, 1940, edition of *Maria Legionis*, the official journal of the Legion of Mary, appeared the first of a series of reprints of talks delivered in Dublin by Mr. F. S. Mitchell. As subsequent articles appeared, it was felt that the matter contained in them was sufficiently important to demand much wider diffusion. Obviously, there was much that concerned the Legion of Mary only, and hence a direct reprint in book form of the addresses as delivered did not appear to satisfy the purpose intended. So, the articles have been edited with due permission, and brought together in the pages that follow with some additional chapters on the nature of the lay apostolate.

Chapters III to IX inclusive are edited versions of the original addresses of F. S. Mitchell, reproduced here by the kind permission of the Editor of *Maria Legionis* who still retains all rights over them, while the remainder of the book is the contribution of the co-author.

If it is borne in mind that many of the pages that follow are really transcripts of talks, it will be understood why the first person singular intrudes itself so often. The editor felt that it was better to leave the addresses like this rather than risk destroying their directness by trying to eliminate their personal tone.

Let it be stated at once, also, that this is not meant to be a critical or controversial book. A point of view is stated in regard to the nature of the lay apostolate with which some may disagree; but there is certainly no intention whatever of criticizing any existing systems or movements. Modern Catholic Action is still in its infancy, and all will benefit by the frank propounding and discussion of views and theories as to its nature, scope and technique. It is only from such discussion that the whole truth will eventually emerge. It seems too early yet for any one movement to claim that it represents the absolute ideal. Just as there are within the Church many hundreds of Congregations of Religious, each with its own distinctive spirit, so, there is room for many different organizations of the laity in the general field of Catholic Action. Nevertheless, there must be an ideal, a norm, after which all will aspire. To outline that ideal and norm is one of the purposes of the pages that follow. Another is to inspire many souls to begin to discharge their obligations as active members of the Mystical Body of Christ and to guide them a little in regard to the techniquie they must follow.

Francis J. Ripley.

Church of St. Francis de Sales,
Hale Road, Liverpool 4, England
October 26, 1947

CONTENTS

		PAGE
FOREWORD	. . . .	iii
INTRODUCTION	. . . .	vii
DEDICATION	. . . .	xiii
I. SATAN REVISES HIS POLICY	. . . . . .	1
II. MODERN ROADS TO CHAOS	. . . . .	24
1. Political Collapse	. . . .	24
2. Social Collapse	. . . .	25
3. Educational Collapse	. . . . . .	28
4. Cultural Collapse	. . . .	28
5. Collapse of Religion	. . . . . .	29
6. Root Causes of Our Failures	. . . .	31
7. The Ideal Lay Apostolic Movement	. .	33
8. Needed a Militant Minority	. . . .	37
III. WHO IS RESPONSIBLE?	. . . . . .	40
1. The End of a Submarine	. . . . .	40
2. Callousness towards Our Neighbors	. .	44
3. "But I Pray for Them!"	. . . . .	52
4. We May Neglect No One	. . . .	55
IV. APATHY VERSUS GRACE	. . . . . .	58
1. The Tragedy of Inertia	. . . . .	58
2. Action with Grace	. . . . . .	63
3. Discrimination Frustrates Grace	. . .	64
4. Christianity's Original Commission	. . .	67

CONTENTS

PAGE

V. WHERE IS THE MAGNETISM OF CHRIST
  TO-DAY? 69
  1. The Dynamism of Christ 70
  2. We Must Mirror the Zeal of Christ . . 74
  3. Challenging the World 77

VI. THE APPROACH TO THE MASSES 80
  1. What Is a Crowd? 81
  2. How to Approach Each Soul 86

VII. THE PARALYSIS OF FEAR 90
  1. A Campaign against Fear 94
  2. Are There Christian Heroes To-Day? . 98
  3. "But What Will People Say?" 102
  4. The Valiant Woman 105

VIII. UNAPOSTOLIC CATHOLICISM AN ANOMALY . 108
  1. Why Are There So Few Miracles To-
    Day? 111
  2. Miracles a Corollary of True Faith . . 113
  3. Confusing the Natural and Supernatural . 116
  4. An Unfortunate Mode of Thought . . 120

IX. MARRIAGE—AT A PRICE! 123
  1. "We Cannot Get Married Yet!" . . . 125
  2. Getting Married for God 128
  3. Demonstrating the Ideal of Marriage . . 132

X. MARKS OF THE APOSTOLATE 137
  1. Is Knowledge Indispensable? 138
  2. Personal Contact the Key to Success . . 145
  3. Sincerity and Simplicity 151
  4. Needless Multiplication of Qualifications . 153

CONTENTS

	PAGE
XI. A TASK FOR CATHOLIC EDUCATORS	157
1. Meeting a Subtle Attack	158
2. Integral Christianity versus Integral Paganism	159
3. Lack of Red-Hot Apostles	162
4. Shirking Our Responsibilities	164
5. A Practical Solution	165
XII. SOCIAL ACTION AND THE CATHOLIC APOSTOLATE	169
1. Work for the Workers	169
2. Catholic Action's Aim	171
3. A New Approach	172
4. St. Paul's Greatness	175
5. Papal Pronouncements on Catholic Action	177
6. Record Low Level of Catholic Literature	178
7. A Challenge to Paganism	180
8. Needed Prayer plus Action	182
9. Fallacy of Sociological Christianity	183
XIII. TRUE DEVOTION TO MARY A NECESSARY INGREDIENT	190
1. Mary the Link between Laity and Priesthood	193
2. Mary Forms Us into the Image of Christ	196

TO THAT VAST ARMY OF
LEGIONARIES OF MARY
WHO, CONSECRATED TO HER
AND IMITATING HER VIRTUES,
GO FORTH UNITED
TO KINDLE EVERYWHERE THE FIRE OF DIVINE LOVE,
TO ENLIGHTEN THOSE WHO ARE IN DARKNESS
AND IN THE SHADOW OF DEATH,
TO INFLAME THOSE WHO ARE LUKEWARM,
TO BRING BACK LIFE TO THOSE WHO ARE DEAD IN SIN,
SANCTIFYING THEMSELVES BY PRAYER
AND ACTIVE COÖPERATION
IN MARY'S AND THE CHURCH'S WORK
OF CRUSHING THE HEAD OF THE SERPENT
AND ADVANCING THE REIGN OF CHRIST,
THESE PAGES ARE
AFFECTIONATELY DEDICATED
AS A TOKEN OF GRATITUDE
TOO DEEP TO FIND EXPRESSION IN WORDS

I. SATAN REVISES HIS POLICY

WHAT FOLLOWS is not, of course, a play in the sense that it is devised for acting on the stage. Likening the inhabitants of the Kingdom of Darkness to human beings, we have tried to present an imaginative reconstruction of a conference they might have held to devise ways and means of countering the growth of the lay apostolate. The place names are used simply as a matter of convenience and have no reference to events that have taken place in those places.

SCENE I

The scene opens in the Office of HIS SATANIC MAJESTY, *who is seated behind his desk. His* PRIME MINISTER *stands before him. The year is 1927. The time 9 a.m.*

Satan. You seem worried this morning, Premier.

P.M. I am, Your Majesty. There is bad news from up above. The Pope is continually demanding that all members of the Church throw themselves into what he calls Catholic Action.

Satan. But what effects follow his words?

P.M. Our latest despatches are gloomy in the extreme. The idea seems to be catching on; the laity are talking about getting active. Meetings are being held; plans are being made. They threaten to overthrow us altogether.

Satan. Not much to worry about so far, then! Meetings seldom get anywhere, and plans rarely mature. Let them talk away, but see that they never translate their talks to action. Our technique must be to keep them talking and planning.

P.M. All the same, Your Majesty, I think it would be as well to call a conference of all our commanders in the field. We could discuss the whole affair and each will benefit from the pooling of ideas. Obviously, if this idea of the lay apostolate, as they are calling it, ever really gets going, it will be a bad day for us.

Satan. There is something in what you say. In any case, a conference cannot do any harm. Let it be summoned for this afternoon.

Scene II

A Conference Chamber in the midst of hell. Satan *is seated on the fiery throne; on either side of him are his* Ministers of State; *in front, sitting in rows, the commanders in the field.*

P.M. Gentlemen, this Conference has been called by His Majesty on my suggestion to discuss the threat to our kingdom which has taken the form in the world above of Catholic Action, or the lay apostolate. The idea seems to be that every member of the Church is to be made to acquit himself of his duty as an apostle. So far, we have been able to keep that idea out of the minds of our respective proteges; we have—very skilfully, I think —kept them arguing about abstruse theological questions; we distracted them by the Great War, and so on. But now the position threatens to become alarming. At last the humans seem to be getting down to things in real earnest. I want you to remember the purpose of this Conference and to avoid the error the humans always make of wandering from the point. We are not here to discuss Communism or the work of any other of our departments; the purpose of this discussion is simply how we can best prevent the spread of an effective lay apostolate. Speak, gentlemen.

America. It is obviously impossible for us to deny the principle that all members of the Church are meant to be apostles. The humans would see through that immediately. But we can utilize all our usual impediments to good—apathy, inertia, sloth, selfishness, love of pleasure, and the like.

Satan. We take it for granted that all of you will apply those old weapons with all the vigor at your command. But the trouble is that the humans realize that those are our weapons. They call them vices. We do succeed with them; we must continue to use them; but we must have something more subtle.

France. I have an idea. Let us tell them to pray.

Several in Unison. To pray?

France. Yes, you heard me—to pray, I said. You look surprised. You are not subtle enough. What I mean is that we must convince people that prayer alone is enough; we must try to make them think they are doing their full duty by praying. You know what will happen. Most of them will not pray at all, and those who do will spend so little time at it that it will be negligible. Therefore, my brothers, let us put all the stress on prayer so that action will be forgotten.

Spain. I second that. The suggestion is well worthy of our French representative. Let us take it seriously and work on it with all the cunning at our disposal. Convince folk that they have only to pray, and they will neither pray nor work.

Satan. I agree. We can consider the proposal accepted. Now let us hear more.

Ireland. In my field of operations they seem to put great stress on devotion to her whom they call the Mother of God. It seems to work, too.

Satan. I *know* it works. I wouldn't be here only for her! We all have to thank her for our present unhappy abode. Nothing would give me greater pleasure than to get even with her. But we must be careful. As the humans have it, "she is terrible as an army in battle array."

Ireland. Yet the matter seems simple enough at the moment. The theologians are simply playing into our hands by disputing about her. The result is confusion for the ordinary mortal. We must encourage them as much as we can.

Satan. There is a lot in what you say. We all know that Mary is the channel by which all graces pass from God to the human race, and that therefore real devotion to her must be proportionate to her position. But we must prevent the humans practising that devotion, and, as far as I can see, the best way to do that at the moment is to concentrate in setting confusion abroad.

Ireland. Yes, that is true. From bitter experience we know that Mary always repays devotion to her. If these humans start consecrating themselves to her, or putting this lay apostolate under her patronage, our position will become hopeless. It must be stopped at all costs.

France. Therefore, we must prompt the theologians to keep on crying "danger," "excess," "heresy," and so on. Devotion to Mary must be kept down. But we cannot attack it directly; therefore, the only way is keep it low and thin and poor, a shadow of what it ought to be. Tell people to pray to her, encourage them to be sentimental about her, but fill them with the fear of going too far, teach them to say what we got the Protestants to say with such success—that honoring her is taking away from the honor due to Jesus Christ. I may say that I saw this particular danger years ago; that was why I arranged for the copy of a treatise by that Grignion de Montfort to be lost.

P.M. Yes, you did well then, France. I think we can trust your experience in this matter. What it boils down to is this: we cannot tell these humans that devotion to Christ's Mother is a bad thing, but we can give them the idea that it is dangerous to go too far with it; at all costs, we must stop them from giving themselves to her as servants, as that de Montfort of yours suggests. I know that, if any of these Catholic Action movements builds itself up on this idea of a devotion to Mary proportionate to the place the Supreme Being has given her in His plans, it is bound to succeed, and that will be a sorry day for us. So, I think we can call that agreed. Any further suggestions?

Australia. As a comparative newcomer to your Councils—I have held my present position a mere couple of hundred years—may I suggest a plan likely to succeed? The Pope's program is being called the "*Lay* Apostolate." Is there not a chance of playing on the word "Lay," and setting up some kind of opposition to the clergy?

Satan. Well spoken for a junior!

America. Hear, hear! In the English-speaking world they are beginning to call the priest, "ecclesiastical assistant." I suggest that we play on the word "assistant," and try to get the clergy—who are notoriously proud of their office—to resent the idea of being subjected to the laity.

P.M. That means a twofold action: working on the laity to get them to have an exaggerated idea of their position, and working on the clergy to make them resent any lay interference at all.

Australia. Exactly. I think we ought to try to get the clergy excluded from the movement as far as possible. It will not be hard to convince the laity that all executive decisions should be taken by them, and that the priest should be there more as a consultant on spiritual matters.

America. As a spiritual watch-dog?

Australia. Yes, something like that. We must soft-pedal the idea that the priest is there to train the laity, too, or inspire them. In fact, I think we have here the makings of a grand idea. It will certainly prevent the movement coming to anything. Without the clergy we know it cannot succeed; and the clergy won't be in it if they feel they are being demoted to the rank of assistant to the laity.

America. And why not, also, foment trouble between the clergy themselves? For instance, between parochial and diocesan authority? The more confusion we cause, the better. In some places we must whisper that this Catholic Action should be parochial, in others that it should be diocesan. All the time the main object of the thing is being obscured, and that is just exactly what we want.

Satan. Yes, I think our policy is clear on that point. Trouble must be stirred up with great subtlety between clergy and laity, and amongst the clergy and laity themselves. On the last point you are all sufficiently experienced. But remember—no sledge-hammer methods. "Subtlety" is the watchword. Anything further?

England. May I add a word? I think I can boast of a large number of creditable performances in the past. If this Catholic Action succeeds, all my good work in bringing about the Reformation will be undone.

Satan. Stop boasting, then, and get on with what you want to say.

England. I think the obvious thing is to spread abroad amongst the humans an altogether wrong idea of the apostolate. The more definitions we can make them play with, the better.

Satan. Excellent. But give us some details.

England. Suppose we get them to confuse, for instance, the apostolate with some of its parts, with

8

the spread of knowledge or the spread of social principles or . . .

P.M. All right. Let us take one point at a time. Let us discuss the possibility of making them confuse the apostolate with the spread of religious knowledge. What would happen?

England. We all know that the real idea of the apostolate is to radiate Christ. It means imparting convictions, passing on to another one's own picture of spiritual things, showing off the beauty of religion without the spirit of controversy or superiority. Obviously, then, we have got to encourage the humans to think they will spread the faith if they are learned, or by argument. Then they will get down to study, and you will all agree that study soon becomes an end in itself, and excludes action.

Satan. Very cute. Even *I* hadn't thought of that one —although doubtless I would have done so before the discussion was over. We must generate a regular fever for knowledge, but at the same time we must convince those who are studying that they never know enough to be apostles, and so action will stop, or rather it will never begin.

England. We must be subtle. We must insist that all this is done in the name of Catholic Action. My technique will be to exalt the apostolate to superb heights and to dwell on the terrible re-

9

sponsibility of those engaged in it and the awful consequences of making a mistake—maybe giving us more companions down here—

France. Satan knows we could do with them.

England. True, but don't interrupt. As I was saying, I shall tell my people in England that, if they go in for being apostles and then make mistakes, they may be responsible for damning souls. That will scare them all off, or at least it will make them start studying and studying and studying, and all the time I will whisper: "You don't know enough yet. Study more."

P.M. Good enough. But don't forget to impress on the rank and file that they know nothing. We know that they know a lot. They haven't been saying their prayers and listening to sermons and reading their pious books and taking lessons at school for years without knowing the heaven of a lot. We mustn't let them think they know enough, though.

Australia. Another idea. We must not let them remember that the people they are trying to win over from us know a great deal less than *they* do. That is not going to be hard. In my territory they talk to one another about cricket and sheep and business of every kind, and they never stop to take a course of study first. But suppose they realized that they are just as qualified to talk religion?

Satan. I see what you mean, although you are not as clear as our more experienced members. The point will be noted: spread abroad an inferiority complex about talking religion.

P.M. We must not forget to make them put undue emphasis on argument. If we can get them to waste their time arguing, we will have done a good job, because arguing more often antagonizes than convinces. I think England is to be congratulated on raising this point. It is likely to prove very effective. If we work on the lines suggested, we will keep the number of apostles down to a handful. No one will ever think himself learned enough—or the few who do will get nowhere, because they will spend their time on argument.

Satan. We are doing well. Can any of you suggest any other means of reducing Catholic Action to inaction?

Spain. Yes, Your Majesty. I think it is clear that we must try to make these humans who are impudent enough to try to take up arms against us by taking part in the apostolate waste their efforts on side issues, or what they like to call red herrings. We must get them to do anything but approach souls directly.

Italy. Our friend speaks from experience. The essential thing in the apostolate, as we know, is the pouring out of its choicest possession by one soul into another. We must stop that. We must divert effort into cul-de-sacs.

Spain. Most of us are adepts at raising the cry of "prudence," "caution," and so on. Even now our efforts have caused the idea to be very widespread that souls cannot be approached directly; that to talk religion is, as they say up above, something that is "not done," that the direct approach will be resented, that each must mind his own business, that charity begins at home, and the like. All we have to do is to keep these ideas alive and work hard on any organization that tries to combat them.

Satan. What all that amounts to is that we must prevent personal contact.

Spain. Yes, principally that. I heard one of my contacts preaching the other day. He said: "The secret of all success with others lies in the establishment of personal contact." I tried hard to distract him, but I was unsuccessful.

P.M. Hard lines, old man. But do not lose heart. One set-back here and there is to be expected. If you look around their world, you will see that we have already succeeded to a great extent. In some places Catholic Action has become a publishing business; in others it concentrates on the radio; in others it is thought to be a matter of talking to crowds.

Satan. Our work should be fairly easy in this respect, because the mass approach is much more glamorous in its appeal. Some men love to stand up and talk; we must encourage the pride of that type. Others love to brag about the numbers of pamphlets or Catholic papers they have sold; let them, but do your best to see that the pamphlets and papers are not used as a means of personal contact. They cannot do much harm if they are delivered impersonally.

England. I persuaded one of my contacts to slip round after dark putting leaflets through doors. I told her it would be much better like that—much safer and less embarrassing for herself. She swallowed it, too.

P.M. Excellent. All of you must note that at all costs you must prevent this Catholic Action concentrating on personal contact. That alone can bring it real victory over us. I have issued orders before that house-to-house visitation by the clergy in the parishes is to be prevented as far as possible. The principle is the same. Personal contact between priest and people is bad for our cause. So is it between members of Catholic Action and ordinary folk.

Satan. I think we all understand that perfectly. Are there any other points?

Belgium. As an officer of long standing, I would

like to suggest that we do something about the liturgical apostolate.

P.M. Have you any detailed suggestions?

Belgium. Yes, several. In the first place we should bring about a general concentration on liturgical, instead of private, prayer. Then we can use that to make them forget the essential thing in liturgical prayer, the Mass.

Holland. How would we do that?

Belgium. Simply by tempting them to concentrate on externals—the rubrics, vestments, chant.

Holland. What is the real point behind this? What has it to do with the lay apostolate? Our anti-Mass department will surely have thought of these points.

Belgium. We were talking a few moments ago about tempting the humans to waste their time on argument. The obvious reason for that is to make them forget that their most powerful weapon for good is the presentation of the beauties of their faith to those who do not believe. And the most beautiful thing in the faith, as well as the most powerful, as we especially have reason to know, is the Mass.

P.M. Then the apostle must be holy, and the source of holiness is the Mass.

Belgium. Quite. Therefore, the point I am trying to make is more important than ever. The Mass is for the apostle both the chief means of self-sanctification and his principal instrument for working upon others. Hence, if we cunningly make him forget the real meaning of the Mass by devoting himself to the externals or trimmings, we are hitting right at the core of his scheme.

Satan. I think it goes without saying that we who have been in this place so long, and have no prospect of release, should always concentrate against any growth in real love or appreciation of the Mass. Since it was the first Mass that took the humans from our sway, anything at all that we can do against the Mass will be more than worth while. But be cunning. Do not start campaigning directly against the Mass; follow the advice of our Officer in Belgium. He has spoken well. Cause confusion between liturgical and non-liturgical prayer; set up factions in support of each; make them concentrate on mere externals and so on.

Belgium. I have another suggestion, your Majesty.

Satan. Let's hear it.

Belgium. I think we ought to foment class distinction amongst these apostles, and get them to increase it amongst the members of the Church in general.

England. How can that be done?

Belgium. Simply by tempting people to start movements restricted to this or that particular class. This is bound to impair efficiency.

England. Surely it is a correct principle that "like will always act upon like," or, as they say, "birds of a feather flock together"?

Belgium. Yes, true enough. But surely the very aim of this Catholic Action should be to combat the divisions and antagonisms in the world, to bridge over and not separate the various classes of men? Its goal is to restore the human race to its ideal unity, modelled on the unity of the Mystical Body of Christ. If we make Catholic Action concentrate on divisions, class distinctions, restricted movements and the like, we are bound to be forwarding our cause. As for your principles, they will operate in any case. A man does not cease to be, say, a worker, just because he does Catholic Action.

Satan. I see the point of the suggestion, and it is quite a good one. You must remember it and employ it as the opportunity arises.

America. May I return to a point that someone made a while ago? It is important for us always to give the impression of exalting Catholic Action. That enables us to insist on so many prerequisites as to exclude any large numbers from the movement.

Satan. What kind of prerequisites would you suggest that we try to make the Officers demand?

America. I suggest that we tempt well-meaning and sincere people to write books dwelling on all the qualities which an apostle ought to possess in such a way as to give the impression that without these qualities one cannot be a successful apostle. We might even get them to develop the technique so far as to issue examinations of conscience for would-be apostles, or to devise schemes for the working out on a percentage basis of one's apostolic quotient.

Satan. I see. You would try to make them assess people according to their appearance, posture, neatness, voice, judgment, knowledge, courage, enthusiasm, sympathy, sincerity, dependability, determination, persistence, and so on?

America. Yes, and I would go further. It is amazing how these things develop. In the course of time we might get someone to demand a daily bath of all leaders or to draw up regulations restricting the use of make-up by the girls. Not only would these things exclude large crowds who would otherwise be working against us, but they would set up barriers between the potential apostles and their contacts.

Satan. Very good. Another point to be noted. Anything that tends to cut down the numbers active against our rule is to be encouraged.

France. There is a further point I would like to suggest. It is that we encourage those keen on Catholic Action to boost schemes before they have been tried.

Belgium. Very sound psychology.

France. Then those responsible would get large numbers of adherents at first, and most of them would soon fall out; the remaining few would be both too discouraged to continue, and too few to form a force.

Satan. Good for you. We must try to prevent any movement becoming so established as to be able legitimately to parade the results it has achieved. If we put into operation all the suggestions we have heard to-day, that ought not to be too hard.

Australia. In spite of my youth, I have yet another suggestion which I consider good.

P.M. We will decide when we have heard it.

Australia. Naturally. It is that we tempt these men to place the means in the position of the end.

Satan. You mean that you think we could tempt them to make the means—that is, the local organization or set-up—an end in itself?

Australia. Yes, it would be easy. We have surely enough experience of the pride men take in children of their own ideas. If we can get them to set up Catholic Action organizations in different places—based, note, on untried plans and falling into all the traps we propose to lay for them—we can play on their pride and get them to refuse room to other and better (worse, from our point of view) organizations.

Satan. You are more cunning than I thought. What you mean, for instance, is that we should encourage those who call themselves leaders to establish systems of Catholic Action in various places, all worked out in theory and never put into practice; we should urge them to gain adherents, and then stick to their plans through thick and thin, even though some more successful system should come along from elsewhere.

Australia. Precisely.

Satan. Excellent. We will do it. Great success seems likely because it is a cunning based on pride.

P.M. Of course, it goes without saying that we will encourage these well-meaning mortals to make their organizations as complicated as possible. Few things kill action so quickly as over-organization. Simplicity is a virtue we must not allow them to practise.

Satan. I agree entirely. Any further ideas?

Belgium. Yes. Why not use the social chaos we have created in the world as an instrument to kill Catholic Action?

Satan. How?

Belgium. By making men concentrate on it to the exclusion of Christ.

Satan. I see. Will you give us a little more light on your plan?

Belgium. Yes. The obvious aim of the apostolate must be to spread abroad the spirit of our enemy, Jesus Christ. Hence, that aim must be obscured. We must get them to identify Catholic Action with the rebuilding of a new economic order in the world, so that men will come to regard the Church as just a natural thing, and a competitor with all the other forces we have brought into being— Communism, Nazism and the rest.

Satan. Good. The result, as I see it, will be that Catholic Action will become vitiated by concentrating on only a small fraction of its object, instead of the whole. We know that the only way they can rebuild the world is through the intense and patient application of the religious system of the Catholic Church. They must never realize that. We must see that they concentrate on just wages, conditions of work, Trade Unions, and other more or less material things, forgetting the one essential—the establishment of the reign of the Eucharist in the hearts of men.

France. But is it not bad for us that the social apostolate should thrive in the world?

Satan. Yes, but it may be the lesser of two evils. If they use up their energy on that, they will have none left for the more important and vital thing, the direct spiritual apostolate to souls.

France. I see, and I agree. My neighbor Belgium has hit on a first-rate idea.

Satan. Before we adjourn, has anyone anything further to suggest?

Africa. Yes. You ought to see that Catholic Action organizations become so bound up with rules and regulations and local customs that they become incapable of flexibility or adaptability. It would be a tragedy, for example, if my contacts were to be able to import a system from, say, Ireland, which would be so flexible in its organization as to be adaptable to their requirements.

Satan. All right. Note that point too.

France. Another psychological point is this. No organization will succeed unless it makes worthwhile demands of its members. Hence, our plan must be to get Catholic Action to be afraid of asking too much lest it lose its members. The results will be precisely that members will be lost and the work done will only be trivial.

Satan. Very good. Now, as time is getting on, I think we can draw this meeting to a close. I will summarize our decisions from the notes I have made.

1. We must use cunning and subtlety at all times.

2. We must get the humans to fall into the "prayer alone" heresy.

3. We must prevent devotion to the Mother of God, especially such as is wholehearted and proportionate to her place in God's plan of Redemption.

4. We must play on the term "lay" apostolate, and use it to antagonize the clergy.

5. We must set up antagonisms between the laity themselves, and spread abroad confusion as to the diocesan or parochial nature of Catholic Action.

6. We must propagate false notions of the apostolate, especially causing it to be confused with the spread of religious knowledge.

7. We must place undue emphasis on study and argument.

8. We must suggest that the direct apostolate is impossible.

9. We must divert the minds of apostles from personal contact, and get them to concentrate on the mass approach.

10. We must make them use a false idea of the liturgical apostolate, one concentrating on externals and forgetting the essentials.

11. We must prevent the Mass being used as an instrument either of self-sanctification or the apostolate.

12. We must foment class-distinction in Catholic Action.

13. We must insinuate all kinds of prerequisites

so that the numbers of apostles will be reduced.

14. We must tempt organizers of Catholic Action to boost plans rather than successful systems.

15. We must play on their pride, and so get them to make the means or system an end in itself.

16. We must cause undue emphasis to be placed on the social apostolate, so that the main spiritual apostolate will be overshadowed.

17. We must suggest over-organization or excessive rigidity.

18. We must advise caution against asking too much of the individual apostle.

P.M. Thank you, your Majesty. Now to your allotted posts in the battle against the power of heaven. It is your duty to try out all the ideas we have discussed this afternoon. The more surely you succeed in getting them applied, the more certain is Catholic Action to fail, and we to triumph.

Exeunt omnes in a blinding flash.

II. MODERN ROADS TO CHAOS

"WHAT IS WRONG with the world to-day? How can it be put right again?"

These two questions are on everybody's lips—in the press, in the queues, in the shops, in the schools, in parliaments, in offices, everywhere. Day after day we read of some new contribution towards the solution of the world problem, and how grave the problem is may be gathered from the fact that a film star's opinion is counted as valuable as that of the savant.

Yet, basically, there is only one answer: the world has lost Christ, and Christ must be brought back to the world.

Analyse the position for yourself. Consider the present failure and you will realize that it is possible to sum it up under five large headings: failure in politics, failure in social organization, failure in education, failure in culture, failure in religion. Not that those headings include everything, or that they are mutually exclusive, but they do offer a fairly reasonable basis for examination.

1. Political Collapse

Few will question that this is an age of failure in politics. Whether we examine our own domestic situation, or probe into the political systems of nations across the seas, or consider the relations between States, we have to admit failure. The history of politics in English-speaking lands is a sad story of personal ambition, graft and intrigue welded together with all the evils of the party system and the absence of any authoritative guidance in matters of religion or morality. In other lands the war has reduced political life to chaos. Everywhere the belief is gaining ground that the State is everything in the individual's life, and that its wellbeing is his first concern, taking precedence over the rights of God, of family, or of individual. In many countries there is scarcely one tenet of Christianity that has not been openly flouted, and in Russia and her many satellites, new and old, irreligion is being promoted with all the power at the command of a ruthless governmental machine. Certainly if you accept the definition that politics is the science and art of securing and advancing the temporal welfare of the nation, you have to admit that politicians have failed ignominiously in our day.

2. *Social Collapse*

The second great failure is the social failure. Expediency and not justice is the motive force in economic as well as in international relationships; in private life self-gratification and greed have supplanted the love of God and one's neighbor. The goal of industry

25

under modern conditions is not the supplying of needs, but the making of profit for further investment. The fallacy is still prevalent that, if each individual will only look after his own best interests, the good of society will follow automatically. In practice, the worker of to-day is almost entirely at the mercy of the good will of an employer, who will not suffer himself to be bound by the demands of Christian morality. In an age of plenty, multitudes all over the world live in want and danger of starvation. The concentration of wealth and all the despotism that goes with wealth in the hands of an ever-decreasing few has rendered the masses of the people helpless. They are beginning to feel that initiative and effort to better their condition are futile, and that even the hope of better things is gradually passing from vision. Human relationships have been supplanted by inhuman, so that the modern factory hand is much less than a man; he is merely a sentient part of the machinery.

On the other hand, we hear far too much about the *rights* of workers and far too little about their *duties*. The Christian idea of work has long since been forgotten with the result that class distinctions are being over-emphasized, not only by the employers but principally by the organizations of the workers themselves. Society is, indeed, organized on a basis of class-war, and management and labor have become two armies drawn up for a bitter battle. Instead, they should be the two main coöperating factors in industrial life.

Turn now to the sacred shrine of the domestic hearth. Modern social theory justifies willful murder under the titles of abortion or euthanasia, the destruction of the family under the high-sounding name of contraception; by its divorce laws it tears asunder the contract of a marriage which has been solemnly ratified before the throne of God. A mother of to-day thinks nothing of complaining of her "bad luck" in being saddled with a second child, and she makes no secret of the fact that the number will not be increased. Millions of pounds and hundreds of millions of dollars are being frittered away on tobacco, drink and the cinema by the very men and women who complain most against the unjust concentration of wealth within the power of a capitalist minority. Young people feel that life is not worth living unless they are always on the move and away from home. Not to have visited the cinema at least once in the week is regarded as a grave omission, and there is no discrimination between the good, bad, or indifferent film. So we could go on. But even such a brief survey proves beyond doubt that in its social, economic and industrial organization the men of the twentieth century have lamentably failed.

3. Educational Collapse

The third failure is in education. There is an almost universal denial in practice of the fact that the primary right to educate rests with the father of the child. For years now the State has been arrogating to itself the responsibilities of parents, so that State education has become the accepted rule of things, and the worst crime of all is that it is a godless education. In fact, the system of public education at present in operation in almost every land is a standing contradiction of all the first essentials of true education, because it neglects to form the child in the knowledge and love of God and in habits of virtue. In spite of all their boasts, in spite of all the millions of revenue spent on it annually, the people of our age have to count education as their third great failure.

4. Cultural Collapse

And what of culture? In the world of thought and intellectual achievement, the men of to-day have receded from a level previously attained. They have allowed their minds to be filled with worthless substitutes which have brought many disastrous consequences in their wake. The universities, founded by the Religious of the Catholic Church and supposed to be the centers of culture, are soaked through and through with the false principles of the new materialism, and Christianity is scorned as a relic of the decadent past. In the fields of literature, of music, of painting, of architecture and of sculpture the same is true. The outstanding masters of literature have been deposed in favor of the modern novel and the popular magazine, vehicles for the expression of the ideals of paganism. It is the exception to-day to find a novel or a magazine which contains nothing whatever contrary to Christian teaching. With regard to music, canned sound has taken the place of human achievement, and a crude imitation of the debased music of the African jungle, deliberately calculated to arouse sensual passion, has supplanted the compositions of genius and inspiration. In painting and sculpture and architecture we find the same trends towards despiritualizing the culture of our fathers. "Religious faith and the idea of God," said a Soviet teachers' journal, "must be replaced by science and the idea of the machine." Is it possible to deny, then, that the fourth great failure of our age has been the failure in culture? [1]

5. *Collapse of Religion*

And the fifth, most basic of them all, is the failure in religion. Apart from the Catholic Church, there is not one single religious body in the world which can

[1] Cfr. "The Theory and Objectives of Bolshevism," by Walter Legge (C.T.S., London).

offer authoritative guidance on vital questions to the man in the street. In view, for example, of the vacillation of the non-Catholic Churches on such matters as divorce and birth-control, it is scarcely surprising that they command few adherents to-day, and that by far the greatest number of our fellow-countrymen do not frequent any church at all. Here, indeed, is the secret of the other four great failures. With Jeremias we may well ask:

> "Hath not this been done to thee because thou hast forsaken the Lord thy God at the time when He led thee by the way? Thine own wickedness shall reprove thee and thine apostasy shall rebuke thee. Know thou and see that it is an evil and a bitter thing for thee to have left the Lord thy God, and that My fear is not with thee, saith the Lord God of hosts" (Jer., ii.17).

But I am not prepared to limit the modern religious failure to non-Catholic bodies. I say deliberately that members of the Catholic Church are failing also, and failing because they are not offering the ordinary citizen a lead along the path towards the return to Christ. Faced with this onslaught of secularism, the Popes in a magnificent series of Encyclicals interpreted modern political and social theories and tendencies in the light of the teaching of Our Lord, but these Encyclicals have been rendered practically null by the passivity and apathy of the Catholic body at large. Although *Rerum Novarum,* the great Encylical of Leo XIII known as the Workers' Charter, was a more revolutionary document than the Communist Manifesto, how many of the Catholic laity have ever read one line of it? What organized and systematic effort was ever made to get its contents across to the working multitudes of the English-speaking world? It has been regarded rather as a prize essay than as the practical directions of the Vicar of Christ on the ordering of affairs vital for the spiritual and temporal wellbeing of humanity.

6. Root Cause of Our Failures

This brings us to the kernel of our answer to the questions we proposed. If the root cause of the troubles which affect humanity to-day is neglect of God, it is obvious that the only real remedy is for humanity to return to the spirit and teachings of God-made-Man. But whence is our race to relearn those teachings, whence obtain that spirit, if not from the one true Catholic Apostolic Church? Hence, the counterstroke of the Church has been the call of all her members to the apostolate under the general title of Catholic Action, and a new emphasis by the Popes on the obligation of every member of the Church to be an apostle.[2]

But it must be noted that, even though the world

[2] Cfr. "Calling all Apostles" (Paternoster Publications, London).

were not so wicked, the apostolic obligation would still be there, for this duty is part and parcel of a full Catholic life. The Church is Christ's Mystical Body, the continuation of the life of Christ upon earth. Therefore, the Church must mirror to men every characteristic of the life of her Head, and especially His zeal for souls. The whole purpose for which God the Son became man was our redemption; His whole life was directed towards the saving of men's souls. That was why He exemplified every virtue during His sojourn upon earth, why He preached, why He suffered, why He chose to remain with us in the Blessed Eucharist, why He sent down the Comforter upon the Apostles, why He Himself appeared to St. Margaret Mary exhibiting His burning Heart. Hence, of all His qualities that apostolic characteristic must be particularly evident to those who examine the Church—and not only the Church as a whole, but the Church as it exists in any place. As the visible Church exists only through its members, it is clear that every individual Catholic is intended to mirror to men something of the burning and practical zeal of the Sacred Heart of Christ.[3]

More of the motives for the apostolate will be found in the pages that follow. For the present we are content to state the obligation in general terms. Obviously, there is room in the Church for a great

[3] Cfr. "A Blue-Print for Lay Action" (Paternoster Publications).

multitude of different movements all qualifying to be included under the general heading of the lay apostolate, but the majority of those that have appeared so far hardly merit the title of apostolate at all. Many of the most publicized are run by small numbers of enthusiastic or paid workers, and are engaged upon work which at best is only preparatory or accessory to the real apostolate of soul to soul— the furnishing of educational statistics and information, the registration of teachers, Catholic education research, providing the Catholic press with news, study, the publication of programs connected with industrial and civic problems, the collecting and classifying of legal information, the dissemination of literature, and so forth. All this is excellent work, of course, but not really of the essence of the apostolate.

Hence our plea that movements be started and encouraged everywhere which are really apostolic, based on the apostolate of personal contact and open to every practising member of the Church. If it is true that every Christian must be an apostle, then the qualifications for engaging in organized apostolic work cannot be such as would exclude any large numbers. Otherwise, a true principle is reduced to an absurdity.

7. The Ideal Lay Apostolic Movement

Whether or not a movement organized along these

lines is official Catholic Action will depend upon the decision of local ecclesiastical authority. The Legion of Mary, for example, which by its character, rapid expansion and almost miraculous results obtained, has proved itself to be the most successful apostolic movement in the Church to-day, is in some places designated official Catholic Action, in others an auxiliary to Catholic Action, and in others simply an approved work. Hence, throughout these pages we shall avoid all questions of organization and confine ourselves to general principles.

By way of brief summary of what is to follow, we suggest certain points which will characterize the ideal lay apostolic movement:

(1) Its object must be the sanctification of its members by prayer and apostolic work.

(2) It must be subject to proper ecclesiastical authority.

(3) It must be based on a sound devotional foundation, embracing a profound faith in the Holy Trinity—in God the Father and the love He bears His children, in God the Son, the Redeemer, and in God the Holy Ghost, the Sanctifier.

(4) It must be truly Christocentric, that is, based on the doctrine of the Mystical Body as explained in the Holy Father's Encyclical on the subject.

(5) It should embrace a devotion to Mary pro-

portionate to the place she occupies in the scheme of Redemption as the channel of all graces.

(6) It must insist on regular prayer as an essential part of the meetings and of the daily lives of the members.

(7) It must give the priest his rightful place as teacher, counsellor and guide of the members, and while it remains a lay movement, its laicism must not become aggressive.

(8) It must carry on an apostolate based on personal contact in a manner that is at once enterprising, effortful, and self-sacrificing.

(9) It must be open to all practising Catholics who are sincere and willing to acquire the spirit.

(10) Its Constitution must be such as to combine the intense order necessary for discipline with the flexibility necessary for a successful apostolate.

(11) It should hold meetings at least weekly, and insist on attendance at these as a first duty of membership.

(12) Spiritual direction should form an essential part of the meeting, which should be designed primarily for apostolic action.

(13) The members must be taught that they are always on duty for souls, a leaven in the community.

(14) Humility must especially be inculcated, because it is both the instrument and cradle of apostolic action.

(15) Each member should be allotted a definite work obligation every week, and be expected to report the following week on how he has carried it out.

(16) The spirit of kindliness and harmony between members must prevail.

(17) The Holy Eucharist, both as Sacrifice and Sacrament, should occupy a central position in any apostolic system, because it is the source of the graces required for action and a powerful instrument of conversion.

(18) Study should always be regarded as a means to apostolic action, and not as the end in itself.

(19) The ideal of the movement should be to establish personal contact with as many souls as possible, good and bad, with the purpose of benefitting all.

(20) All work should be allocated and controlled by the movement.

(21) Politics and class distinctions should be non-existent within the movement.

(22) Vagueness of every kind should be avoided, especially in the allocation and performance of work.

(23) The work done each week should be really substantial.

(24) The spirit of supernatural charity should pervade the whole movement.

(25) The idea of the movement should be to train its members to pass on to others the picture

they themselves have in their hearts of the Faith and all it means to them.

(26) The direct approach to souls should be the first consideration.

(27) The ultimate aim should be the patient application to the ills of humanity of the religious system of the Catholic Church.

The pages that follow do not claim to be a full treatise on the lay apostolate; they deal only with certain important aspects of it, and especially with those which do not appear to be sufficiently appreciated or understood.

It is not within the scope of this work for us to lay down in concrete terms the exact details of an apostolic organization. Rather we prefer to deal with the lay apostolate in general, which, of its nature, is capable of embracing many different societies each with a different spirit.

8. Needed a Militant Minority

We do suggest, however, that there are very few parishes indeed in which it is not possible for the priest to gather round him a group of apostolic layfolk who will be pleased to allow themselves to be trained in the spirit of loving zeal for souls, in courage, in humility, and in all that is necessary for the conducting of an apostolate amongst their fellows. There are many people who are filled with a downright anxiety to work for souls; they simply desire to be shown the path and to be given the support of others. They realize the need for action, or at least they will respond if taught to realize that need; they are capable of action, but they do not know how to go about it. Give them training, give them organization, give them encouragement, and you will have set in motion a force that will grow mighty in the course of time and sweep away before it the poisonous weeds of sin in ever-increasing measure. More than that, you will find that more and more of the laity will become vitally interested in their religion; they will grasp something of the idealism that lies latent in the doctrine of the Mystical Body; they will be fired with the desire to work for and love all mankind in Christ; they will begin to think in terms of service, to make great sacrifices, and even to embark on a course little removed from the heroic. "Revolutions are made," said Stalin, "by militant minorities."

All we ask is that the suggestion made by Pope Pius X, and quoted by Abbot Chautard in "The Soul of the Apostolate" (p. 151), be generally adopted.

"Happening to be one day in the midst of a group of Cardinals, the Holy Father said to them:
" 'What is the thing most necessary at the present time to save society?'
" 'Build Catholic schools,' said one.
" 'No.'

" 'Multiply churches,' replied another.

" 'No again.'

" 'Increase the recruiting of the clergy,' said a third.

" 'No, no,' replied the Pope. 'What is most necessary at the present time is to have in each parish a group of laymen at the same time virtuous, enlightened, determined and really apostolic.' "

III. WHO IS RESPONSIBLE?

1. The End of a Submarine

(Somewhere off the coast of New England, a submarine lay on the ocean bed, battered, broken, unable to reascend. In its hull five men were bravely waiting—their voices still calm and devoid of fear. The talk reverberated from the metal shell which formed their prison.)

Lieutenant. What time is it now, Skipper?

Skipper. 4.15 a.m. You asked me the same question, Lieutenant, exactly six minutes ago.

Lieutenant. And why not? There isn't anything else to do.

1st Sailor. Whatcha kickin' about, Lieutenant? Submarine's one whole wheeze—nothing to do but sit down and draw extra pay.

2nd Sailor. Join the Navy and see the world, with buckets of dough to buy yourself a good time!

3rd Sailor. (*grumpily*). Shut up, you guys—you're using up the air.

2nd Sailor. Yeah! What air? Me ole lady got me into this business because she said them airyplanes was fallin' all the time. She sure has got me down about as far as I can go!

Lieutenant. My head's just bursting.

Skipper. Easy now, easy now, Lieutenant.

2nd Sailor. It's all very well for you to talk, Skipper —you haven't a wife and kid to leave behind. I'll go mad thinking of her. I can see her face now, when she hears the news.

Skipper. It's a good job the lights didn't go when the tub cracked up.

Lieutenant. Yes, I'd have lost my nerve long ago in the dark. As it is, they are nearly gone. My head is bursting.

Skipper. Easy now, easy now, Lieutenant.

3rd Sailor. The Coast Guard will get through.

2nd Sailor. Not a hope, buddy—them blokes is too busy chasin' dames!

1st Sailor. Bully for them. Wish I was with them.

2nd Sailor. Yeah! And what about the brush-off you got from that last blonde you had?

1st Sailor. Gee, that baby was a hep-kitten—just my idea of a real classy dame!

Skipper. Dames! Dames! Dames! Do you guys ever think of anything else? I only wish we had Dinny and that mouth-organ of his. It's the only time I ever really wanted to hear him play.

1st Sailor. He's playin' the harp now on the other side of this "tin-can." He was a great guy; always ready to slap a tune on top of our blues.

3rd Sailor. That rescue party *must* get through.

2nd Sailor. Aye! And so will the Marines.

(The three sailors chat in low tones together. Skipper and Lieutenant do likewise for a couple of seconds, then the Lieutenant's voice rises.)

Lieutenant. .... at the Gardiners' Party in New London, Skipper. You must remember her—she wore the white dress with the red trimming.

Skipper. Oh! I remember her now. She had a brother there, didn't she? Surly cuss that played Contract so well?

Lieutenant. That's the one. The last time I saw her was the night before I went away. There's something about that girl that makes it hard for me to go now.

Skipper. She is beautiful, all right, but I think she's too old for you.

Lieutenant. It's the way she wears her hair. Funny thing, I was reading a letter of hers when this crash came. She's sweet, Skipper. Gosh! just my rotten luck this should happen now.

2nd Sailor. Any rum left, Skipper? My throat's awful parched.

1st Sailor. The only thing I want is a big glass of beer. Wasn't it a swell night we had before we put to sea? The booze runnin' like Niagara. And remember the singing! Wasn't Dinny hot on the mouth-organ? We didn't think we'd never be on shore again.

2nd Sailor. I wish the sea would bust these walls

and wash away the pain in my poor dome. It's giving me gyp. *(He splutters.)*

Lieutenant. My head's cracking open, too. What time is it now, Skipper?

Skipper. It's half-past *(cough, cough)*, half-past, past—

Lieutenant. Funny, too. Always fancied myself as a family man—when I got promotion *(cough)*. Funny the way everything works down to dollars in the end!

Skipper. O.K. for some guys. Never chanced it myself. This air stinks.

1st Sailor. Heck, Skipper, here's the water in! Look, the little leak over there!

2nd Sailor. Maybe it will wash the air. *(Laughs hysterically.)*

Skipper. Steady, you guys!

3rd Sailor. Save the air! Save the air! SAVE THE AIR! *(He speaks in a rising hysterical crescendo.)*

Skipper. Pipe down, sonny; it makes no difference.

Lieutenant. Yes, Skipper, I intended my son should serve Uncle Sam in the Navy. Wonder what he would be like.

1st Sailor. What about that rum, Skipper?

2nd Sailor. It'll make you sick.

3rd Sailor. That rescue must get through. I know it will, do you hear! It'll get through *(slightly panicky)*.

2nd Sailor. Aye, and so will Father Christmas.

Skipper. No harm in hoping anyway.

Lieutenant. Skipper *(splutters)*, my head is horrible *(raises his voice)*. I just can't stand it.

Skipper. Hold on, son, hold on!

Lieutenant. O.K. I'm better now.

2nd Sailor. What day is it?

3rd Sailor. Sunday, you dope.

2nd Sailor. Me ole lady and the kid always do Central Park on a Sunday. Gee! I hope she won't let him join the Navy. Junior's a fine kid. Wonder if he'll miss me much. *(He splutters.)* It can't be long now.

Skipper. Well, there'll be no one to mourn me. Can't remember my father. Mom passed over years ago. Wonder why I was so keen on the sea. Don't regret it, though—it was a good life though tough in spots. Never keen on dames, either, since a girl I was fond of gave me the hard knock.

1st Sailor. Water creepin' up, Skipper.

Lieutenant. Say, you guys, what about getting it over quickly when the water rises?

Skipper. Not for me; while there's life there's hope. Life to me is a series of sensations, some good and pleasant, others bad, but I don't mind whether they are good or bad. I just want to experience them— even this headache for as long as possible; and so I would rather die a lingering death than be snuffed out at a moment's notice.

2nd Sailor. Golly! What a slant on life you have, Skipper! Me! I don't want to live unless there's somethin' good cookin'.

1st Sailor. Sure! Life's only worth living where there's plenty of dames and tin.

3rd Sailor. Well, there ain't no dames here *(cough)*.

Lieutenant. What time is it, Skipper?

Skipper. Well, Lieutenant, we'll never again know the time—my watch is stopped! It stopped at . . . *(cough)*.

(All cough and splutter—then there is silence.)

. . . .

What is the idea of the foregoing strange dialogue which rings so out of tune with what you are accustomed to in a spiritual book? It portrays five men in a submarine on the ocean bed waiting for the coming of Death in grisly form. He is near; actually in the punctured, poison-filled "tin-can" with them. Already his fingers touch them, probe their vitals.

The scene is adapted from a much longer episode in a current novel in which there are forty men instead of five. The necessary compression into much smaller compass squeezes out most of the characters and a lot of the color and effectiveness of the original.

In the latter, all the forty men did some talking. They reacted in different ways, but all reproduced the same general note as in our less vivid presentation —that is, *not a single one spoke of God*, and, so far as the narrative gave any indication, *no one was thinking of God or of a hereafter*.

Fervent meditation on "Dames, Dollars and Drink" forms a fantastic preparation for Death.

You say: "Only a story!" No—more than a story. It is the projection into print of the mind of the author, depicting men as he has seen, heard and known them. That is how he figures the men of this world would deliberately occupy their last few moments on earth. Admittedly—or at least he would probably concede—his picture is not balanced; it does not mirror *our* world. But it does represent *his* world. As he is to some extent typical of other writers and other men, so to some extent is his picture typical of the real world. Not that we need labor this point, for we all know how bad things are. Therefore, it forms shocking contemplation. For if there be a gleam of faith in a man, it will be fanned to flame in those decisive moments. If there be in the soul any fear or love of God, it will then betray itself. Certainly, that would apply to the vast bulk of Catholics. Yet, I have known a few who made their exit in the manner of the crew of the submarine —and worse!

Now transfer that process of thought to the world at large. Run the eye of your mind over the great cities. In each of them, there are multitudes living *that life*—a life in which God has no part, which no ray of faith or hope or true charity illumines. They are born into the great adventure of life, and their pilgrimage towards eternity proceeds. But according to what principles? Nothing better, nothing else, than the principles of the moth facing a line of candles. "Dames, Dollars and Drinks" are all they know about or care about. Then enters Death, and here in charity we must refrain from adding a fifth alliterative link.

Surely some one is to blame! Surely we are not intended to remain spectators of that spiritual chaos in the same helpless way that we would survey the mad churnings of the ocean! Multitudes around us are typified by those five poor souls whom the introductory dialogue has staged for us. Their spiritual darkness is more intense than that of the ocean bed outside the wrecked submarine. Either they have never been taught to know Christ; or if they once were taught, they have not been retaught or rewarmed. If they were eagerly sought out, they might be terrifically different; for even the slightest contact of grace works strange wonders, and may mean the difference between a soul's loss and its salvation. But they have not been sought out with the intent to effect those changes. They have been left forlornly to the process of action, interaction, and reaction with other victims or agents of evil like themselves. And how right thoroughly that process does its work!

If the public knew of that submarine's plight, what frantic efforts would be made to help it! In a flash the whole world would be aware of the tragedy, and in a sort of agony would follow its developments. Every material aid would be mobilized, and men innumerable would be willing to place their lives in jeopardy by desperate attempts at rescue.

But when it is only souls that are at stake, what a different tale there is to tell! Most people, even the good Christians, appear to feel for souls at large no responsibility whatever. Or if they do admit some responsibility, they then proceed by pleading difficulties and special circumstances to dilute that responsibility to such an extent that it ceases to be a real one at all. Obviously, responsibility must not mean something which is the opposite to responsibility. Neither must it terminate in mere feelings, study, writing, reading, radioing, and that sort of "preparation" which never gets down to the job. The approach to souls must not be made so scientific a technique as to be generally impracticable, or so indirect as to bypass its objective, or so gradual as never to reach it.

Approach must be nothing less than the sort of straight-forward wholesale going to souls which the pages of the Gospel picture for us. For, despite surface appearances, the conditions of to-day are much the same as those of the Gospel times, and the Gospel is not otherwise out of date.

2. *Callousness towards Our Neighbors*

Has this anything to do with us? St. John Chrysostom asserts that it has everything to do with us: "Christians, you will render an account, not of your own souls alone, but of the souls of the whole world." What a shock for us if we were to consider that seriously! But perhaps the Saint meant it to be taken seriously, as reflecting the mind of the Lord and echoing His words. For that is precisely what the Gospel seems to say: that on the shoulders of other men, jointly and severally, lies the responsibility for each of those almost infinitely numerous poor souls (as for the five sailors on the submarine) who are now living godless lives, and who will in due course pass through the Dread Portals in that "tin-can" spirit.

Those sailors in the submarine were far from being the worst in great populations—although possibly one or two of them may have been as bad as they come, real bad! But mainly their sins were those of ignorance and passion—which does not, however, alter the fact that those sins, like a reeking deluge, cover the face of the earth. And this sort of wrongdoing shades into worse. There are the multitudes whose motive-power is malice: the perpetrators of enormities; the exponents of the Black Mass and other dealers in the Black Art; villains whose villainy has paid them; those who would commit a murder for a trivial sum; the doers of wholesale cruelties and injustices which make blood and tears run in rivers.

Then there is the uncountable world of those who are respectable but who have no faith—which is to be worse off than the greatest criminal who has in him some spark of the supernatural.

Then there are others who have some faith, but not *the* Faith: no Mass, no Sacraments. By comparison with those other grimmer specimens, this class looks good, and we even find ourselves applying the word "holy" to many among them. But do not ignore that "hard saying" of Our Lord's which includes such persons:

"Amen, amen, I say unto you: Except you eat of the flesh of the Son of Man and drink His blood, you shall not have life in you" (St. John, vi. 54).

In many places over the world, the foregoing categories would comprise as much as 95 per cent of the population.

Even to us, with our blunted sensibilities, all that is painful to visualize. What must it have been like

to our beloved Lord—who saw all and felt fully—
when He allowed that same awful contemplation to
overwhelm Him in the Garden of Olives?

"A very appreciable time passed before He
could subdue the instinct of holy horror and submit Himself to His Father's will. All the tragedy
of the Agony is summed up in this desperate strug-
gle. Sin was about to close with Him. He fore-
saw the hideous hand-to-hand fight, and He was
afraid. Presently, as soon as the abominable contact is brought about, the strife will be so cruel and
the effort to resist the embrace of evil so frightful
that He will sweat drops of blood. Then, van-
quished, outflanked, invaded, steeped to the very
marrow in the infamous torrent, He will bow His
Head in the shame and unbearable disgust of His
condition." [1]

Now suppose St. John Chrysostom—and the Gospel—are right! Suppose that we, arrived at the Bar
of Eternal Justice, are accused in respect of the distressing manner in which those poor sailors in that
"tin-can," and the millions whom they typify, spent
their last moments? What are we going to reply to
that terrifying interrogation? Should we try boldly
to bluff it out: "Am I my brother's keeper?" That
cry sounded fine during life, and all the hard-boiled
ones mouthed it and acted it. But if we do, it will not
serve us. For the answer will be simply "Yes," strip-

[1] Bolo, "Tragedy of Calvary."

ping away all pretense and defense and leaving us without a word to say. For all the time we knew in our hearts what the Saint has put into words. We were aware that Our Lord depended on us who had Him to bear Him to those who did not have Him. Without the ministry of one man, He is not given to another—so that indifference and inactivity on our part end inevitably in tragedies such as the submerged submarine and its like.

But perhaps we are able to give a more respectable account of ourselves: "Those things constitute an impossible situation. I deplore it. But what more can I do about it? I am working for souls in my own place, and thus through the 'machinery' of the Mystical Body I am reaching out to the souls who are otherwise inaccessible to me."

That is better. It admits responsibility and shows a willingness to shoulder it. But is that degree of shouldering sufficient? How can it be? For if it were, it would sanction a localizing of faith and Christian effort to the places that already possess those things. It would mean the leaving of the more needy places for ever in their existing condition.

3. "But I Pray for Them!"

Then there is that other rejoinder: "What can I do but pray for those unhappy places and people? And that I do."

You assume that such praying completely discharges your responsibility because of the difficulty—or, as you would put it, the impossibility—of reaching farther out. But I suggest that you cannot thus emancipate yourself—and for two reasons: one practical and minor, and the other of vital principle.

First of all, I ask: "How much do you pray? For do not speak of prayer at all in this connection unless you mean something serious."

Prayer is commonly treated as a soft way out of a duty. "Let us pray" is either a pious formula—not meaning recourse to prayer at all; or else it is a disproportionate, insignificant contribution. But even if it be substantial, does it discharge your responsibility? Except in so far as you are specially consecrated to the life of prayer, I do not think it does. For that again leads logically to the standing aloof from physical contact with those places and problems, an attitude very different from that of the Gospel, which is essentially an attitude of going and doing. Our tendency, almost irresistible, is to fight shy of that physical contact, because it can be so difficult—or, as we tell ourselves, impossible.

Prayer must never represent escapism. Prayer is not supposed to be an excuse, or something into which we relax. It is the prelude to, and the necessary accompaniment of, action. It is the dynamic power behind action. If rightly used, it will lead to action and bring action to fruitfulness. It is like the electric current which is made operative through a mechanism. Action in human affairs might be compared to the necessary place of water in Baptism or of the bread in the Eucharist. So, action no less than prayer is demanded in respect to all those problems. We are human beings, made of body and soul; and both body and soul must strain towards those sinful necessitous souls. Prayer is the operation of part of our being. The remainder of our being must cooperate appropriately. There must be some tangible act or touch, one that can be called physical, between us and those Christ-starved souls. Naturally, that action must be pitched to maximum intensity and display itself in effective ways. But in the event that effective action does not appear to be possible, then some action is called for—in the last resort even a feeble gesture, even an unconnected or in itself futile physical reaching-out—like going out and running, or such a symbolic act as the preaching of St. Francis to the birds and fishes.

Does this seem utterly ridiculous? Possibly it does. But there is method in its madness, for it will save us from what would otherwise happen in almost every case—that is, total and largely inexcusable inaction. Then, having established it as a first principle that we must do something, our sense of the prudent and economical will shape our action into effective forms; so that we will not have to continue for long that type of action which I call "symbolic."

4. We May Neglect No One

It is not enough that the confessionals and altar rails should be open to all Catholics, and that the tough ones have a chance of being dealt with in prisons and hospitals. That is only thinking in terms of the Catholics. Moreover, it is but the minimum approach to the latter, and rather amounts to their approaching us. To encounter us, they have to come to our territory; whereas the essence of approach is that we go to theirs, and there seek them out, one and all. We must go into the depths and the dangerous dens to seek them, even into their more inaccessible places —such as into their palaces.

"Oh, but all that is rank impossibility in this modern world! Impossible!"

In saying so, you forget to speak and perhaps even to think as a Christian. Our attitude to the "impossible" must be conditioned by the following considerations: firstly, the spiritual, which tells us that with God "no word shall be impossible," and that by faith and effort we can reverse the natural impossibility; secondly, the psychological, which should teach us that, if we grade something as impossible, we virtually make it impossible; thirdly, we must note that the divine command to seek out every soul was not limited by a sub-clause about their welcoming us or being amenable.

So, the idea is approach on any terms, at any cost. If we leave a loophole, even though it be far smaller than the proverbial eye of the needle, our ingenious weakness will enable us to wriggle out through it. So, there must be no loophole—which means that, even in the face of situations which seem genuinely hopeless, that action which I call "symbolic" must be staged. When that step, which seems so futile, is taken, it will place a more effective one within our reach, and then still another one. Just as each new peak which the climber scales shows him a higher one, until the ultimate one stands up ready for conquest.

5. An Essential Ingredient of Action

But I must not take one ingredient of action so much for granted as to omit its mention. For it is essential; it is the Marian element. Without this latter, it is possible to act prayerfully and energetically, and yet to accomplish nothing of worth. For Our Lady is part of the principle of fruitfulness. Our Lord does not please to be fruitful of Himself. He did not come on earth without Mary. Likewise He insists on her action as the condition of His revolutionary entry into souls. Without Mary, accordingly, the greatest strivings will only end in sterility. With her, on the other hand, every effort brings its due fruit, while heroic acts effect the miraculous, and therefore can reach out to and solve the pitiful things that the submerged submarine stands for.

IV. APATHY VERSUS GRACE

1. The Tragedy of Inertia

IT SEEMS TO ME that the supreme need of the day is to bring home to every Catholic that on him rests the positive duty of going out and seeking conversions to the Church.

What is the Church? The Church is a society in which Jesus Christ lives, and which exists for the purpose of bringing Him to all men. If in any place the Church were not leading that life, then it would be untrue to its mission. Were the Church in any place to do no more than minister to those already in its own ranks, it would only be in partial being there. It would have turned itself into a chaplaincy; and Christ never intended His Church to be a mere chaplaincy.

But the Church is made up of its members, can only operate through them, and stands or falls in them. It follows that from each individual member the Church requires responsibility for and coöperation in its work. But one cannot say that such are being shown to-day in that primary department of the Church's action, the winning of converts. It is not realized by the rank and file that it is their bounden duty to bring the Faith to everyone—without exception—who does not possess it. That conviction of imperative duty being absent, and the difficulties—interior and external, natural and supernatural—being many and great, what can result but deadly inertia?

That inertia does not necessarily mean indifference. Actually it can be found coëxisting with real, downright anxiety to win people to the Church, just as in the heart of a paralysed man may be found an ardent anxiety for action which physical restrictions deny to him. In many cases that inertia springs from a natural cause. If you study people, you will find what an extraordinary severance can exist between the powers of cogitation and those of action, so that the most terrific action may take place in the mental department without ever being translated into physical action. That gap exists in everybody. It is narrow in what we would call the man of action. It is pretty wide in the average man. In a certain proportion of people it is a yawning, almost unbridgeable chasm.

Inertia can proceed from other causes—the fact, for instance, that people require to be shown the path, that they require one another's support. One may realize the need for action, one may be capable of that action, and yet not know the way to go about it.

The remedy for that inertia lies in the application of organization. In other words, you must set up a bridge which conducts people over that gap, an organization which holds a certain idealism and subjects them to a sweet pressure. Then, in the measure they submit themselves to that pressure, they will find themselves doing things. Results that have come already are heartening, because they seem to prove that it is possible to organize the entire community—and any community—in the same way and to get always comparable results. Consequently, the horizon of hope which stretches before us is illimitable.

I fear we can take it as an unfortunate fact that the ordinary run of unorganized Catholics do not recognize themselves as having any duty in this particular direction. In fact, some people go very violently into reverse and conceive it even to be an incorrect thing to do anything. They make a virtue of inaction. They clothe it in sugared phrases: "We must not unsettle other people! . . . If they are in good faith, let us leave them so! . . . We must respect the beliefs of others!"—and so forth.

This phraseology is familiar to us all. In practice, its effect is deadly. What does it mean but that we are to try to convert nobody except those who convert themselves? This is what is called an "Irish bull." And, like the same animal in the proverbial china-shop, that virtuous inaction works havoc in the Church. It tones down its mission; it perverts its meaning. It turns to mere domestic purposes the infinite ocean of grace which is meant to irrigate the universal desert of unbelief. Then—final tragedy! —that domestic stream tends to dry up. Actual experience proves that we do not hold even our own members; they slip away between our fingers. But what else could happen? Our practical indifference towards those arid souls outside has earned disaster for ourselves.

2. *The Anomaly of Prayer Alone*

There is another phrase which many use to soothe the holy pang which they may feel from hearing repeated references to the teaching of all men. They say: "We pray for those outside the Church." We pray for them! Of course, that is to the good—if we do pray for them! Sometimes that is no more than a conventional phrase. But even when it means something, I wonder who told those people that their prayer alone suffices? We are in the world, and action is called for from us. And to the extent that we do not *act* along with prayer, we do not get results. Again, what do those persons who talk about praying mean exactly? How much prayer do they mean? Are they going to spend two or three hours of an evening praying? No. Those people mean an

Our Father and Hail Mary—perhaps only a Hail Mary!

Then there is that other plausible but crippling thought which whispers that you are not qualified to make an approach to others, and accordingly that you are exempt from trying. But who is qualified? The priests, of course, are. "But surely knowledge, ability to argue, etc., are essential?" Here you must distinguish between the instructing of converts and the seeking of them. The former demands knowledge; the latter only zeal. Recall what happened in the early Church. If this is going too far back for you, reflect on what took place last year in the one mission station of Nairobi—where native apostles brought in 1,000 catechumens.

So beware of those opium-like sayings which pull with inertia instead of against it, and which neutralize the program of action which fell from divine lips. I do not say that those cautious phrases are always wrong. Sometimes they may refine your action. But doubt them whenever they tend to paralyse it. Remember, too, that even a fine plan of action may cause inaction. For the ideal solution may not immediately be practicable. Then we piously hold ourselves excused from doing anything, instead of working bravely at the second-best—which eventually brings us to the best. As has been said, the better is often the enemy of the good.

3. Action with Grace

Action is paramount! You may challenge this and say that grace is paramount; and of course it is, inasmuch as absolutely nothing can be accomplished without grace. That is a fact about which we have no illusions whatsoever. We realize fully that everything depends upon the Lord. But in a sense, too, it does not; because that grace will *always* be given if it be *properly sought;* then its action will be automatic. We can take the gift of grace for granted. What is in doubt is our own coöperation, not God's. Thus, we can hark back to what I have already said and once again urge on you—that effort is paramount. Simple effort must come first; after that, supreme effort, after that—and only after that—enlightened, artistic, brilliant, genius-like effort. Nothing is expected of anybody except what he has got. A man who is not a genius cannot elicit qualities that are proper to genius. Nevertheless, his misdirected, clumsy, stupid effort will be equal to the effort of the genius, if it is all that he can give, and if he does not fall below the genius *in the faith and love he puts into his effort.*

If the maximum of effort is forthcoming, then grace will come—overflowing, conquering, miraculous grace, like any of the highlights of the past. We had an example of that in the case of an air-raid shelter in Liverpool where two Catholics were saying the Rosary. A land mine fell beside the densely packed shelter; yet, in circumstances that were patently miraculous the people all escaped unscathed. The Catholics had finished the fourth decade of the Rosary when the mine dropped. Then when they pulled themselves together and realized that they were still on earth, their first thought was to give out the fifth decade in thanksgiving. The sequel was that twenty persons handed their names for instruction. I suppose many believe mass conversions to be impossible at the present day. Not so. Make the proper claim on the Lord and He will respond with big things.

4. Discrimination Frustrates Grace

Another principle is that the number of your contacts should be the main consideration, and not the emphasizing of quality or promise. This sounds very odd, I know, but it is logical. It seems to me that the concentrating on quality and on alleged promising people is a dangerous mirage which will lead us astray. Who are we to judge as to who are the promising? Sometimes things work out very differently indeed from what they promise—sometimes the very opposite: the eligible and the promising never fructify, while the unpromising often yield rich fruit. A multitude of eminent cases attest to that. Only the Lord can judge the heart. None of us should venture to do so. Our job is to seek out all, and to bestow on all unbounded, heroic effort.

I cite the following examples which history records of unlikely-looking people who entered Christ's Church: (1) the Thief on the Cross; (2) W. H. Mallock; (3) Oscar Wilde. On the other hand, there are notable examples like Gladstone and the late Lord Halifax, who stood on the border and appeared to be about to come in, and yet died outside the Church.

Moreover, the most unpromising of material exhibits a higher ratio of conversion to the Church than other sections of the population. Some time ago an able young Mohammedan Indian stated at a meeting that the remedy for the divisions and antagonisms of India was to take a leaf out of the Russian book and to atheize the country. I reflected to myself that of all who were there he afforded the very least prospect of conversion. Now consider this: he was the first of all that body to come into the Church! So much for human judgments!

Here is another example. A group of us were recently discussing a distinguished man, who had come to us labelled, so to speak, by a person of great discernment as an outstanding soul who was very near to the Church. Our group could discern very little of the spiritual in him at all. Who was right? It only shows how impossible it is to form an accurate judgment of people's qualities—let alone of their souls. Therefore, we should be slow to indulge in that sort of classification.

The more numerous the contacts, the more numerous will be the conversions. There is a mathematical ring about that, but it will work out true. But there is a higher principle than that which requires the multiplication of our contacts. It is the one I have already mentioned—that through us the Church must reach *every* soul. So, it is a case of the carrying out of a mission, not the following up of anything that may seem promising. And even if those contacts seem vain and worthless and barren, and even if by some prophetic glance we knew them to be vain, still we are to follow them up. Why? Because God has said so! I was much impressed once by an account which I read of a French missionary in China. He had been a very distinguished layman in France. He left all, became a priest, and went out on the mission to China. Apparently he was working in a bad spot. He did not accomplish much during all his time there.

Somebody asked him if he were getting results. He said: "No."

Then the inquirer, with an eye on his past brilliant career, suggested to him that he was wasting his talents and that he should seek a more promising field of labor.

His answer was: "I am not here because of past success nor because of prospective success. I am here because of the command that the Gospel be preached to every creature."

5. *Christianity's Original Commission*

That noble remark contains a lesson for all. Incidentally, it puts the mission of the Church in a nutshell. Grasp that nutshell, and note that, when that commission was originally given by Our Lord, there was no suggestion of any process of selection, or of promising contacts, or of non-approach to those who had other beliefs. The commission was made comprehensive. Approach was to be *to all*.

If any misgivings still exist regarding those to whom we are to go, or the way in which we are to go, and if we find ourselves thinking in terms of selection and circumspection, then we must think of that other command: "Go out quickly into the streets and lanes of the city, into the highways and hedges, and compel those you find to enter in."

There is not much of the element of discrimination in this commission. We would be topical in calling it a "mopping-up operation." Furthermore, there is even the note of capture and compelling. Where are the niceties in all that? There are none. What is painted for you is someone burning with zeal for the Lord's Kingdom going out into all sorts of places, getting after all sorts of people (many of them queer enough), and with a gentle insistence inducing them to come in.

Again, the image of the Church that is put before us in the Gospel is that of a ship. It is a fisherman's craft, and the fishing therefrom is done by nets—not by rod and line; nor is it directed to the princely salmon or trout alone. That casting of a net is the undiscriminating gesture that the Church must always make, and that we, as units of the Church, must imitate. The net is cast, regardless of what is going to be brought up in it—big or little, good or bad. We must even throw it out where there is little or no prospect of anything coming in. For you will remember the incident in the Gospel which is commended to us—the casting of the net in faith where all previous castings had been fruitless. You know the sequel. The net was filled to breaking-point with great fishes.

V. WHERE IS THE MAGNETISM
OF CHRIST TO-DAY?

THE LIFE of the Church is the life of Christ continued. In a measure the same can be said of the life
of each unit of the Church, every one of us. We
poor, weak creatures are only able to reproduce that
life in parts—in broken fragments, I might say. But
the main idea remains the same: it is our mission to
carry on in the world the life of Christ as best we can,
making Him live again in our own ways and circumstances.

Of what kind was the life of Christ which the
Church is intended to continue in the world? It was
a lowly, very hard life, a frustrated life, contradicted
even unto persecution—carried to the extremest limit.
But we must not for one moment think that there was
no other side to it. There was. Taken as a whole,
His life was one of confident strength, and its lowli-
ness and sufferings only served to set off that fact the
more brilliantly. It was a life full of color and character: so dazzling as almost to overwhelm the people
about Him; so striking that many to whom He spoke
but a sentence left all and followed Him; so compelling that even gained second-hand—by which I

mean through mere written accounts and after a long lapse of centuries—the very thought of Him has been able to drive people to follow Him and to suffer grievous things, even as He did and merely because He did.

1. The Dynamism of Christ

The essential feature of His life was power. He dominated the elements, made the dead to live again, and in every other way rose superior to the impossible. Even His mild speech thrilled with that same tone of power—the Scriptures quote for us the bystanders' comment: "He speaks as one having authority." To use a word which seems foolish applied to Him, He was indeed devout—rapt all the time in prayer. But, side by side with that, He was *dynamic* in the fullest sense of that abused word; He radiated force. Everything about Him possessed character; one cannot read a word about Him without realizing what an abyss yawned between Him and any other person—which, of course, is only what we should expect. His influence made itself felt in every way— by His personal magnetism and by the shock of His miracles. He drew the eyes of all to Him; He impelled them to listen to Him, to follow Him about in great numbers. Men simply could not be indifferent. They had to take sides one way or the other— for or against Him. Certain we can be, beyond anything else, that in the whole history of mankind no other man ever made such a personal impression upon the people around him. To use a modern phrase, no one ever made such a hit as did Jesus Christ. No other man ever will or could. Call up before the parade of memory the great figures of history, and you will realize that all of them have feet of clay. There is a saying that no man is a hero to his valet; but Christ was a hero to His valets. He had no feet of clay.

If my original contention is true—that the mission of the Church reproduces the life of Christ in all its phases—then obviously we must find the dynamic note pervading, dominant in, the life of the Church. Disguised, no doubt, it will be by reason of the fact that there is diffused among a great body of people, and with much base admixture, what He held united in His own person. But even though disguised or dimmed by human weakness, the qualities of Christ must shine forth in His people if He is really living in them. Therefore, it would be a very bad sign if the Church in any place were living practically unnoticed or not bothered about, too colorless even to attract disfavor or persecution. Obviously there would be something deplorably wrong there.

But you may retort: "What about the lowly and obscure life of Christ?" I answer that we must look upon the life of the Church—just as we must take the life of Christ—as a whole, even in each individual place. Just as we see that the grand and the challenging was the dominant characteristic of the life of Christ, so must it be in the life of the Church —and that in every place and in every community of the faithful. That sheerly dynamic note simply must be present in some form or another.

It would be a tragic thing if, in any place, the actions of its members toned down the Church to such an extent that men looking at it could discern nothing of the characteristics of Christ: nothing virile, appealing, inspiring, conquering, grand; nothing but an organism that is a slave of its environment, something that has made terms with the world. That would be a fatal thing for us as a body, and for each one of us; for we grow weak with the Church. We are the organs of the Church, the cells of the Church; it lives through us. For better or worse, we contribute to its life. That is a breath-taking responsibility. How unutterably dreadful it would be if those acts of ours, which are supposed to have such a great purpose, were to cause men to see nothing of might or beauty in the Church, so that they judge it to have fallen below even worldly levels! Woe, woe to us then! For in that day and place the Church would have ceased to attract, and even its own people, those born in the fold and nurtured in the Sacraments, would fall away from it like needles fall away from a de-electrified magnet.

Recently a discussion took place about a certain large body of people who are educated, intelligent, idealistic and Catholic, but who could not be described as interested in, still less enthusiastic for, the Church. Their attitude was rightly described as one of cynicism, and that cynicism was analysed as being a compromise between faith and contempt. Those people had the faith, and the natural inclination to practise it. Yet, they had in their hearts conceived the idea that the Church was a stodgy, rather weak product—stuck in the trenches, so to speak, and without a solution for any of the great problems. We know that view to be the opposite to the truth, and we are reminded of Chesterton's classical remark that Christianity has been found difficult and not even tried. But still the position becomes distressing and dangerous if such an idea tends to gain a foothold, especially at the present time when *action* is idealized and idolized, and when great things are being dared and done for purely worldly ends. That sort of temporizing between accepting the Faith and rejecting it cannot last very long—only about one generation, I would opine. Inevitably the next stage will be that of non-practice.

73

2. *We Must Mirror the Zeal of Christ*

But is not that miserable attitude all too common in the world to-day? Look and you will find that irreverence towards the Church is most terribly in evidence inside as well as outside the fold. In his Encyclical "Mit brennender Sorge," that doughty, mighty man, Pius XI, refers to it and prescribes the remedy—none other, he insists, but

"... the closest union of apostolate and personal sanctification for those to whose hands are committed the keeping and increase of the Kingdom of God. Only in this way can it be proved to the present generation, and especially to the adversaries of the Church, that the salt of the earth has not lost its savor, that the leaven of Christendom has not become stale, but is capable and ready to bring to the people of to-day who are caught in doubt and error, in indifference and perplexity, in weariness in believing and in separation from God, the spiritual renewal and rejuvenation of which they stand, whether they admit it or not, in greater need than ever before. A Christianity in which all members watch over themselves, which strips off all mere outward show and worldliness, which takes the commandments of God seriously, and proves itself in love of God and active love of one's neighbor, can and must be the pattern and leader to a world sick to its very heart and seeking for support and guidance, if unspeakable misfortune and a cataclysm far beyond all imagination is not to burst over it."

How every word of that should echo responsively in our minds! Our sacred duty, mark the Pope's words, is that we must prove to this cynical, unbelieving world that the salt has not lost its savor nor the leaven become stale. That is our Charter.

I repeat that the visible Church has its existence only through us its members. Without us it is only an abstraction. Only through us can religion be shown forth as the dominating, captivating thing it really is. Religion is Christ, and no more beautiful thing than that can be dreamt of. Yet, it is only by us that it can be realized. Therefore, each one must show some line or part or feature of the living Christ, so that together we may, like a cinema projector, cast that radiant thing on to the screen of life.

Hence, we must rise superior to our environment, no matter what the difficulties may be. We must dominate it—if necessary and with His help, by the sheerest miracles; and we need never fear that even these will be lacking, if needed. We must make men look upon religion; we must make them wonder; we must make them admire. We must break through that cynicism of theirs, so that those who had been scoffing will set themselves to pray.

When we find people cynical, we must not be overhasty to condemn them. Rather must we reason out the "why." The answer to that "why" may form a condemnation of ourselves. For cynicism is not altogether an unworthy product. In its essence, it is disgust, despair, disillusionment. An idealist who is disappointed may become a cynic, but the idealism has not been destroyed. It is merely submerged. It can be brought to light again.

Similarly, criticisms of religion often have their roots in disappointment or misunderstanding. There are many headlines of devotion in evidence which are false and ugly, and which prejudice people against religion. Take one, for instance—that conception of religion which is known by the expressive term of "chapel-hunting." Those who denounce the latter are not necessarily—as many Catholics possibly imagine—making an attack on religion in general. In reality, they are attacking a libel on religion.

What exactly is this "chapel-hunting"? It is a form of piety which is divorced from the love and service of our neighbor, and even from the details of everyday personal duty and honor. Look around and you will see the type to which that opprobrious title can be fairly applied. There they go, visiting the churches and apparently assiduously praying there, but justifying themselves in no other department of life. That lopsided tribe is not uncommon. In some places, for want of anything better, it is generally supposed to represent the authentic "streamlined" model of advanced religion. As a natural result, the popular mind is biased against the whole idea of devotion; so much so that, when it calls a person a "saint," it means to imply something not pleasant. Thereby the status of religion is impaired, its standards are lowered and falsified; with the inevitable consequence that the standards of the world hold unchallenged sway. That is disastrous. It must not be. Those low, false ideals must be replaced by a Christianity which, as Pius XI says, "takes the commandments of God seriously and proves itself in love of God and active love of one's neighbor."

3. Challenging the World

We can challenge the world only by overshadowing what is there at present. As Christians, we must rise far above the merely respectable, the worthy, the ordinary. We must in our own life exhibit the true standards of religion. That manifesting of the Faith in its lustre and its might must embrace every department of human existence from Pontiff to Cæsar. Every day of our life we must challenge the world in every interest it has; and every faculty and energy we possess must be mobilized in that clash. We must outvie the world, outpace it, outlast it, outlove it, *in everything*—in science, in art, in business, in sport, in achievement of every kind. If we do not, we are not transmitting the spirit of Catholicism. We have to overpower, to overwhelm, to overmaster by sheer quality. If we do this, we will make the Church shine in the world as Christ shone among men. We will make the current standards look drab, cowardly, mean, miserable; so that the Church will attract idealism, and men will turn to the Church with all their hearts, just as men were drawn to Christ in the days of His earthly career.

And there is not merely question of harnessing the best that is in us in the service of the Church. There is far more at stake than that. It is this. When we thus place the best that is in us at His disposal, Our Lord takes hold of what we give. He lives in it, and He exhibits Himself by it, and He will use it divinely for His purposes; and by divinely I mean out of all proportion. He does not merely utilize that contribution of ours, which at best is feeble. I have said: *He lives in it Himself*. It is not we who work, but Christ who works in us. To use Father Faber's phrase, "He mixes Himself up with us." He magnifies our petty efforts to strange dimensions; and ordinary, well-meaning persons find to their amazement that they have been grasped by His power, and availed of for His own most vital purposes; so that the fate of persons and continents—aye, of generations—is made to hinge on their activities.

But have I been forgetting something? In all this

talk about our destiny in Christ, I have only once used the name of her who is, as St. Thomas says, more Christian than all other Christians put together. But, of course, she is to be inferred in every word that I have spoken. By God's arrangement she is vital to that Christian destiny. She is inseparable from everything that belongs to religion. No grace is gained or given otherwise than through her. In all our work and in all our plans we must be mindful that he who builds without her builds in vain. She is not the foundation of the building, but she is an essential part of it. She is not the complete mixture of holiness, but she is a necessary ingredient. Devotion to her does not exempt us in any way from virtue or effort, or from anything else that we should be contributing. But without her, all our thought and effort and planning and everything else will be sterile. Not Christ, but the spirit of the world, will live in us.

VI. THE APPROACH TO THE MASSES

APOSTLESHIP IS a special note of the Church; it is inseparable from Catholicism—inseparable not merely in the life of the Church as a body, but in the life of each individual member of the Church. No one can be a full Catholic without being an apostle.

Apostleship, moreover, views bringing the full riches of the Church to men; therefore, logically, to every one among them—to every person. This means that we have to seek out the person even in the top-back room, and try to bring to him or her all the spirituality that one would find in an advanced book on the subject. But you object that this is fantastic—a rushing to extremes. Admittedly it is, in the sense that a great deal of such spirituality will not be understood or accepted by the people to whom we would bear it. But how can we decide how much and by whom? At least, it must be tendered. Each person has a right to be offered the fullness of the Christian heritage.

If we are going to essay a task like that, it is plain that there is a lot of work waiting for somebody! Indeed, it is a superhuman task. We are talking in terms of the impossible. But reflect that with God no word shall be impossible. If we but set about the task in the reasonably right way and with a reasonably right degree of effort and fidelity, then something beyond natural expectation must happen, because it is the work of the Lord and no mere work of our own that we do. The fact, moreover, that a work is beyond our power forms no excuse for our not attempting it. If we only attempt what we can perform, where exactly does God come in?

1. What Is a Crowd?

The quasi-impossibility of the above program of spiritualizing everybody is due to the fact that you cannot spiritualize men in bulk. The basis of this work must be the individual and persevering touch of one warm soul on another soul, what we call by the technical name of "contact." Each person is a separate and distinct problem; yet, we are obsessed by the contrary idea. All the time we think along mass-production lines, and look on it as a fine thing to get people into crowds so that we can deluge them with oratory or printed matter. It is not realized that in the measure that the personal "contact" weakens, so does real influence. According as men become a crowd, they escape from us. Here is a beautiful expression of that truth, as stated by G. K. Chesterton in writing of St. Francis of Assisi:

"He saw the image of God multiplied but never monotonous. To St. Francis, a man was always a man, an individual—he did not disappear in a crowd any more than in a desert."

But there lies the trouble to-day. We allow people to disappear into the crowd. We allow the crowd to keep us from the person. That is my present theme. I want to write about crowds. What sort of crowds? Any sort of crowd at all—in the street or gathered together in any place. It matters not whether they be passing by, watching, or waiting. I just want you to think of people gathered together in crowds. The uninterested eye flickers over these crowds—unreflectingly; but in the mind of St. Francis of Assisi, or any other apostle, these crowds are no mere mass of faces and bodies; they are made up of individuals, each one representing a priceless soul.

Here, as in many other ways, the children of light are less expert than the world. The politician never sees a mere mob. He sees individual voters, each one of whom he has to cultivate. He studies the characteristics of each person, for the sake of exploiting him. What about the three-card man on the race course? We know well that he sees no mere mob, either. He searches the face of each person that passes, trying to pick out the "suckers." For him the crowd has disappeared, and individuals are there instead.

Similarly, to the interested Catholic eye no crowd should be merely a crowd. It is an assembly of souls—each one of them (no matter what brings them together, no matter what type they are) needing mothering. Every single one is a problem, not alone in time, but stretching into eternity. Most of them, as you watch them, are just drifting along, doing nothing in particular, while plenty of them are more or less destructive. Yet, each is a world in himself, greater by far than the material universe in which we live. Each one is a supreme masterpiece, because God has brought forth his soul directly by a miraculous manifestation of His creative power. Hence, we can be positively certain that no soul is ever just like any other soul. Reflect that the tiny corrugations on the tips of your fingers are unlike those of any other living person. Now, if such is the conduct of God in relation to a thing like a fingertip (which is a thing of little consequence, and which God did not produce directly but through the ministry of one's parents), what is to be imagined of the human soul?

So, what a tragedy it would be if we were to forget that a mob of one thousand people is in reality one thousand souls, each one with immeasurable possibilities for good and evil, for itself and for all others!

Each one is a seed of power without limit for good, but with the capacity also to ruin, and unfortunately more inclined to fill the latter rôle than the former.

There they are in a crowd vitally, peremptorily, in need of this mothering of which I speak. But where, O where, is the apostle who will try to make the personal contact with them which would germinate those latent seeds and stimulate them to an infinite flowering?

Just think of them—any crowd; think of their lack of spiritual development. Even most of the Catholics in that crowd have no more than a child's knowledge of religion—and that possibly half-forgotten. For remember that at the age of 14-16 the vast majority of them severed their connection with the process of education. Whatever amount of religious knowledge had been painfully drilled into them by that age, represented for only too many of them a high-water mark; and the tide has been going out ever since! What are most of them doing in so far as religion is concerned? Probably they attend Mass on Sunday and receive monthly Communion, if they are good; if not so good, Mass without the monthly Communion. But in what way is that Mass heard? The great majority assist without the slightest advertence to what it is. To them it is merely a ceremony. Sometimes, no Mass even. They may say brief morning and evening prayers. They never hear a sermon; the fact that a sermon is added to a Mass would mean that they would make a point of hearing Mass elsewhere. Then, after that exhausting (!) spiritual exercise on a Sunday, the world reigns supreme in their lives for the rest of the week! They never read a spiritual book. You could say in truth that they were trying to dodge the Church for the greater part of their lives.

Of course, for many there is a counterpoise, and that is their homes. Each member of that crowd has his or her private life. There, various good influences may touch them; yet, for a great number of those who form the crowds that we have been considering, their homes are merely dormitories—just places where they sleep. The rest of the time they are—in crowds.

While they are in these crowds, we cannot get at them, and yet eternal things depend on our establishing contact with them. Every day the cord of life of some among them is severed. Out of this world they pass into eternity. We trust it is to a happy eternity; but certainly it possesses little of the fullness which it should have, because the great majority of them are not going into eternity as saints. That much is certain, and the tragedy of it is (as someone has said) that to the mind of God the saint—and not the average person—represents normality. In other words, anybody who is not a saint is sub-normal. Father

Faber says that a saint is worth a million ordinary people. By that arithmetic, many a big crowd is collectively worth only a thousandth part of what God would regard as a normal person. That vast army of souls are realizing but a fraction of their possibilities. Each one is a potential world—yet, it is only playing the part of a clod of earth!

The heart of St. Francis of Assisi, or of any other apostle, could not look with equanimity on that spectacle of great numbers dodging their divine destiny. How must Our Blessed Lady look on those crowds! She is the Mother of each individual soul comprised in them. She must be in anguish at their necessities, and her heart must yearn for someone to help her in her work of mothering them. Be sure of this much— that, if anyone volunteers to help her in a wholehearted way, she will support his efforts with her power. Let us offer ourselves in that wholehearted way. Let us study these crowds. Let us try to evolve a technique which will turn those crowds into individuals, and thus enable us to establish contact with their souls.

2. How to Approach Each Soul?

Take, for instance, the movie crowds. This very evening if you walk along the central streets, you will see a long queue stretching out from every picture theatre; every picture theatre will be packed to the doors. Think again of the football crowds, the boxing crowds, the race-going crowds, and the crowds at the "Dogs," the fancy-fair crowds, the dancing crowds, and the non-Catholic crowds. What about all these? What about the saloon crowds, and the sort of crowd that seems to be doing nothing at all except lounging about, loitering around, just putting in the few hours between now and the time when they have to go to bed?

These are great problems. But somewhere there is the answer to them all—if only we will think, and then have the self-confidence to propound the thoughts which will rise up in our minds. Example, they say, speaks louder than exhortation, so I offer an example.

Some years ago a Catholic announced to me that he was busy constructing a book-barrow. With permission, he intended to place this barrow on the public streets. In due course the article was completed, rolled out, and stationed at a street corner, where ever since it has been a conspicuous landmark. That was a notable contribution to the problem of the crowd! Thousands upon thousands of people have been drawn to that barrow and to its fellows, like the moth to the light, and we hope that those human moths have been duly singed. Many spiritual words have been spoken to them, and many religious books have been politely forced upon them; and if they thought upon the former and read even a small portion of the latter, vast good was thereby done. In addition, many of those that did not stop must have been stirred to think.

You know the story of the simpleton who spent a long time gazing at a wheel-barrow, and then exclaimed: "It's wonderful—the works of a wheelbarrow!" With greater accuracy and with reverence I apply the same words to that street-corner barrow, which ushered in a new work, broadened the apostolic technique, and disintegrated an impervious crowd into its vulnerable human atoms.

We must not let a crowd conceal its problems from us, nor let it intimidate us by its seeming toughness, nor by its size—even though it be very great, while we are few, or even one lone visionary. The difficulties may be such as definitely to place the task outside our compass. But so much the better. "Hopeless" is a hallmark if looked at from the proper angle. Through our slight—but none the less necessary—coöperation, God will show His inexhaustible ingenuity and power. Consequently, if we knock, the door of inspiration shall be opened to us, and then if we seek a way, we shall find it. Of this I am certain, just as I am certain that God wills that the infinite riches of His Heart be brought to all people everywhere. He will walk with us, and fill our hands abundantly with those treasures of His, if only we will prove our willingness to distribute them.

But if, on the other hand, we start off by passing a vote of "No Confidence" in ourselves, we shall not seek; we shall not knock, and the door will remain closed.

VII. THE PARALYSIS OF FEAR

WHY IS IT that many who possess, as we know them to possess, the capacity to shine in one way or another, make so little effort to use it or to develop it? Why, for instance, in a discussion about even a most interesting subject, can only one in fifty be induced to come forward and say anything? Yet, everybody has ideas on the subject, and is well capable of expressing them. What is it that stands in the way? It seems to me the answer is: "Fear." Call it whatever we like, the basic reason is fear, common fear. In the life of everybody without exception that very thing, fear, is playing a dampening part, and it tends to play a destructive one. In many cases that natural tendency is offset by circumstances which press in the opposite direction. Take, for instance, the armies of the world. In them it is largely overcome by discipline. But where this does not operate to neutralize the action of fear, fear exercises its baneful influence over people's lives and characters. It leaves them like seeds which can expand a hundredfold, but which, by reason of lack of heat or moisture, do not germinate. If that is a fact, it constitutes a tragedy. It means that mankind is realizing only a fraction, perhaps a small fraction, of its possibilities. If so, what a loss! Conversely, it means that the life which could emancipate itself from the restraining grip of fear, would accomplish very great things in itself and for the world. That is an intriguing possibility. It is worth all the attention we can give it.

The lay apostolate must recognize the importance of courage, and put very prominently and very forcibly before those who take part in it the need for that virtue. It must insist that, as the ordinary soldier must have courage as an essential of his very soldiership, so must the apostle have courage, and that the apostle without courage is of little use to the movement. The importance of moral courage must be spread. If human respect were permitted to work untrammelled, lay action would for the most part be reduced to nullity. The disastrous effects of human respect must be countered.

But there is an element of danger, it seems to me, that, from the stressing of the evil of human respect and the necessity of combatting it, it might be concluded that there is only need for courage in that particular form. One might think that outside the religious or devotional part of one's life there is no need to be concerned about demonstrations of courage —and, in fact, that courage is only a secular or worldly virtue. Such a view would be a complete misconception. For there should not be for the Catholic such a thing as a non-religious or non-Christian part of a Christian life. We are always on duty; nothing falls outside the ordinary Catholic life. An apostle who is only an apostle during a few hours a week is an absolute failure; the other hours are really the more important if only in the sense that they are the more numerous. We are not Catholics merely during the time of our prayers. We are not to be apostles only during the time of our official apostolic duty. The spirit of apostleship must dominate our whole life. If, therefore, we leave out the courage which imparts virility to the secular part of our life, we are not really apostles during that time. For courage is the soldierly, the Christian, quality. It ranks first in the sense that it is the test of all the others. As the rose root must produce the rose, and the lily root the lily, so must the apostle flower in courage. One may object: "What about prayerfulness, what about sweetness?" Of course, we must possess those things, but they must have the fibre of courage in them. Otherwise they are fictitious virtues. They wilt under trial. They can stand no test.

Yet, of such fair-weather fabric are our lives. Generally we live them in the shadow of fear—fear of every sort of thing, usually fear of failure. That is why we will not get up and talk. We are afraid that we will be laughed at, that we may make fools of ourselves. And besides fear of criticism, there is fear of poverty. Innumerable people live through their lives on a certain low level because they are afraid to face the risks that are incidental to climbing. That low level holds no possibilities of any kind, but, of course, it is safe. Fear has many other forms. Fear of death—some are obsessed by such an abject fear of death that to them might truly be applied the title of that film: "Each dawn I die." Fear of disease —people will not go into certain places or do certain things because they are afraid they may catch something. In the case of a vast number fear of disgrace exerts a particularly powerful influence. But in every case it is fear, fear, fear—fear hiding itself under all sorts of guises but, at bottom, common fear all the time! In some cases the things feared are so remote and so unlikely that what is at work is really nothing more than the "fear of fear," as Seneca describes it. Thereby we are hedged off from our wide possibilities. Most of our dreads are purely imaginary. But, real or imaginary, they are stunting our growth. Fear destroys innumerable fine things in germ. On every life it exercises its blighting influence. Sometimes favoring forces enter in to neutralize that influence. In an organized apostolate, for instance, one will experience such a force. It will enable the individual member to overcome the various fears and reluctancies which beset the path of duty. The system of the organization will lift him superior to fear.

If that be so, what a tragedy if he should narrow down the sphere of apostolic duty, so that for the couple of hours in the week he is a hero, and for the balance just one of the common, fear-ruled folk! No, just as the apostle must always be on duty, so must his fearlessness overflow the banks of his purely apostolic employment and inundate his whole life.

1. A Campaign against Fear

But it is not enough to make resolutions and to hope for the best. We must conduct a deliberate campaign against the operations of this fear. In its character as human respect, we do understand it, and we do campaign against it. All spiritual books suggest expedients to that end. I will mention just a few. One is the wearing of a religious badge. That is an excellent means of countering human respect, which, briefly defined, is the fear to manifest our religion publicly. Then there is the blessing of ourselves at meals in public places. If we are taking a sandwich in a tavern or in some similar place, where such an act is bound to attract attention, we should not be afraid to bless ourselves. One of the finest men I know has told me that the performance of that little act originally cost him an awful lot. Then there is the question of the Angelus—or the touching of the hat when passing a church, especially when we are in company with people who may look curiously at us because we show that little mark of respect. Note: we are afraid even of being looked at! In the life of St. Philip Neri you will find some striking examples of his determination to root out that sort of thing in his disciples. He had many of the young nobles of Rome as his spiritual children, and on these he used to impose the most bizarre things. For instance, he made one young scion of a noble family tie a fox's tail on behind and thus adorned perambulate the streets of Rome. You can imagine what a terrible experience that was for the victim. To that proud type of man death itself would almost be preferable. Therefore, that victory over self was a great victory —falling nowise short of real heroism.

Here is another interesting example of that kind of heroism. It is not without its funny side, but it shows the way strong souls set out to deal with a great evil when they understand it is an evil. A close friend of mine, one of the holiest and most characterful men that I have ever known, was under the direction at one time of an eminent saint. That director had uncompromising ideas in regard to instilling the spirit of courage or virility into his subjects. The following was an order that my friend received on one occasion:

"You are to go out into the streets of your city and beg a penny."

Yes, those were the unbelievable words he heard,

and my friend, who was a very well-known figure indeed in the city, nearly passed away. Try to put yourself in his place. Courage, I can assure you, he had. He had the courage of ten stout lions, but at the ghastly prospect of the task suggested even his great heart almost failed. But "almost" is the saving word—he bowed to the command. For a day or two he almost sweated blood while he mentally acclimatized himself to the ordeal of going forth. He had fevered notions of donning a false moustache, or of otherwise trying to disguise himself. But he reasoned that such would not be playing the game in the Spartan spirit which was intended. So he put on his overcoat, turned its collar up, and pulled his hat as far down over his head as he felt he might in accordance with the spirit of his commission. Then off he went to a church, stood in the porch, and to everyone who entered or went out he spoke the conventional beggar's formula:

"Spare a copper for a poor man."

As he afterwards declared, he went through the tortures of the damned for fear (as was quite likely) he would be known. Consider how someone, having recognized him, would hurry off to say to others: "I did see him, with my own eyes I saw him. He must have gone stark, staring mad." That would make his position in the city very difficult, to put it mildly. It added to the torture of this thought when some abused him, telling him he ought to be ashamed of himself, an able-bodied man like him to be begging. Eventually one woman gave him a halfpenny. But that did not fulfill the contract. At this stage he eased his nerves by seeking fresh fields and pastures new. He moved on to another church and took up his stand in the porch there. After he had suffered there for some time, a very poor man sidled up to him and said:

"I am poorer than yourself, but here is a penny for you."

With fervent thanks—and clutching that hard-earned penny (subsequently cherished as a precious memento)—my friend went off home. Think that out in all its bearings, and you will find in it an act of heroism which I do not think many would be capable of.

Now, that very same sort of attitude which we realize to be necessary towards human respect, that is the universally aggressive attitude, the determination to face and fight it down for the sake of God and for the sake of religion, that must also be adopted by all in the "secular" part of their lives in regard to the appropriate sort of fear that shows itself there. That attitude becomes imperative in the case of an apostle, because courage has to be his profession and because he cannot be a level-road person. He is aiming at sanctity. The definition of sanctity is heroic virtue, and heroism means the defying of fear, the rising superior to fear. Therefore, if sanctity is real sanctity, it must show itself in the form of courage. If it does not, then what looked like sanctity is not sanctity —it is a fictitious thing. If someone you know prays the skies down, but is not prepared to show courage when and where required, then his sanctity is unreal.

2. *Are There Christian Heroes To-Day?*

But here we must make a few distinctions. Heroism is the setting aside of fear when it stands in the way of something that must needs be done. Must we always stamp on fear when it rises up in us? Are we bound by our Catholicism to do so? Of course, we are not. For fear is an elementary human instinct. It is a signpost, a warning, and it is a very important thing that we should possess that instinct. If we had it not, we would be all killed in less than no time. Fault only lies in giving in to it when we should not give in to it. Suppose somebody defies me to swim across a tricky, current-swept channel, which is more or less outside my powers. Am I supposed to go ahead in the teeth of my natural shrinking? Needless to say, I am not. Or someone may challenge me to dive off a twenty-foot spring board. I have not got the skill for that dive, so at once the danger-signal of fear shows itself. Am I obliged to disregard that signal? What does my Catholicism tell me to do?

It tells me that I am to do nothing of the kind. Again, suppose someone wants me to loop-the-loop in an aeroplane, and I am afraid—am I supposed to throw that fear to the winds in every sense of the word? Of course, not. Or take a topical example. During a bombing raid, am I supposed to walk out in the streets merely in order to prove my courage? I am not. That would be without purpose; it would be sheer bravado, foolhardiness. It would be a nobler act to ignore that challenge and all others like it. But the very moment that duty and principle step into the transaction, things become quite different. What was bravado before is bravery now. That foolhardiness has become fine living. Dangerous living may be a duty, and then we must not be held back by fear from doing what duty tells us should be done, however awful its aspect may be, and though the danger signals of fear fly at the top mast. But why pick out these extreme examples, such as bombs, aeroplanes and such like? When Our Blessed Lord was talking of a test, He picked out an even more extreme one. He specified the laying down of our life as the acid test of the quality of our love. Are we prepared to lay down our lives for duty?

When we want to excuse ourselves for weakness in the face of fear, we take those references to venturing and laying down of life as a kind of pious talk, or as counsels of perfection which do not apply to us at all. That view is not correct. It is absolutely essential that we be prepared to stand up and face whatever may betide when there is more than a personal duty—when there is a duty on behalf of religion in general. It is of extreme importance that religion be a virile thing—a tough thing, in fact—though most people do not think that way in regard to religion. Religion must be the toughest of things, and the people who are practising religion should be tough, essentially tough. I do not mean "tough" in the modern American sense of the word. The toughness I mean includes in their proper proportion ingredients like sweetness and gentleness. These latter ingredients must, of course, be there, but they must be founded on and fortified by strength of character. I cannot but feel that there is an overstressing in religion of the importance of sweetness, and that the impression exists that the strong things must yield to it. Not so. Take those two Saints, St. Jerome and St. Paul. They were both hot-tempered men, strong of temper and strong of speech. They were tough men, and yet—because they were great Saints—we can be assured that sweetness was a significant part of their make-up. But toughness had to be there. If we do not see to that, then we are earning for religion the reputation of being a soft thing that only softies practise. We are creating the impression that the legionaries of Satan are the really virile people of the world; whereas the opposite should be the case. Imagine how destructive to the interests of religion such a popular misconception would be. Its first effect would be that upstanding young people (who place special value on courage) would look upon religion as effeminate, and would only practise it by stealth if they practised it at all.

If in our ordinary lives we set ourselves to do anything worth while, fear will automatically rise up in front of us. If fear does not present itself, we are either freaks or we are leading a low-level existence; very probably we are shirking the grim and worthwhile things of life. If we are not constantly encountering fear on our road, almost certainly we are not trying to lead high-level lives. If we start to climb a mountain, the atmosphere becomes rarefied as we proceed. Our breathing becomes difficult, and our heart starts to labor. A painful sensation takes possession of us. In the same way, when we start moving upwards in the spiritual life (by which I mean the whole life lived from the Catholic angle), we run into the rarefied atmosphere of fear.

What is to be our rule of thought in those moments in which both body and soul are chilled, resolution falters, and excuses swarm? It is that we must try to exclude every consideration but the one: "Where lies the path of duty?" Is it our duty to go ahead? If it is, and if we be virile people, then we will go ahead. We will crush within us that instinct of fear to which most people yield. We thereby press on to our destiny, while those others that shrink back from fear-barbed duty, miss perhaps the main road of their life.

When a minor fear presents itself to us, we should counter it in a wholesale way by comparing it with the worst. We should say to ourselves: "This is not a life-and-death matter. But even if it were, it would be my duty to see things through. I must accept death or I play false to my soul." Confronted in that powerful, challenging way, fear is almost extinguished. Thus reduced to the realms of the ridiculous, it no longer has the hold on us that it had, and we go boldly on. It is an excellent thing thus to contemplate the worst and then deliberately devote oneself. Face up to duty in its extreme aspect, and then the minor timidities shrink into insignificance.

3. *"But What Will People Say!"*

In all that I have said, I am not talking in terms of physical fear alone, but of fear in a wider sense. I am thinking of all sorts of fear. There is another type of fear that has a great intimidatory power—what I may call human respect in the secular sphere, that is, fear of public opinion or mob-rule. This is a peculiarly hard thing to stand up against in the mass-production world of ours. It requires abnormal force of character, especially in those who are placed in positions of government or control. Usually, such persons play up to the mob-spirit (which is not a good spirit), instead of trying to educate this spirit and master it. Consider, moreover, how the very best among us are dominated by the herd-instinct of our own particular class or trade, or by some code that we happen to be in thrall to! Some things in these codes are commonly enough very wrong—things which only benefit that particular class, things which are directed against the common good. Yet, we conform to them on the grounds that everyone else is doing them, and that therefore it is excusable for us to follow suit. We do not see in such yielding to fear a betrayal of honor—which in very fact it is. Various examples will come to mind. Every calling has these black spots in it, and many estimable Catholics yield to these things. Take the case of sport: a footballer plays as a man, not as a Christian. In business a Catholic is the tradesman, not the Christian. Thereby both sport and profession are debased to the level of thought and conduct of the natural man, so that eventually they become corrupting influences. Always the excuse is the argument that all the others are doing it—an argument which should be resisted because it is not right, and because it is but fear that argues thus. Evils are removed only by people bravely standing out against them. It always takes one man to stand out—and that man may be victimized. He may be boycotted by his fellows, and no harder thing exists than to render oneself a pariah in one's own class. If we cast our minds back in history, we will realize what that conscientious opposition has oftentimes entailed—a man's life reduced to hell, in many cases death. It takes a very noble person thus to stand up against the mob. But if a man fails to stand out, he must not disguise the issue by fine phrases or in any similar fashion. The real issue is fear: fear versus honor, fear versus duty, fear versus religion.

One may say: "Surely, if I am going to lead a life of that kind, always taking the higher level and always fighting fear, morning, noon and night, what a terrible life that is going to be!"

That is true indeed, and we must remember, too, that fear is not only a thing of the present moment. Fear casts its shadow far ahead—over whole years. It can be a dreadful thing if one is making a fight against it. I know that only too well, because I myself have lived in an atmosphere of fear for whole years. It may corrode a man mentally and physically if he sets himself to fight against it. It is going to mean a very, very hard sort of life—almost an intolerable existence. But were we sent into this world to have a sort of sweetmeat existence? On the contrary, we were sent to tread hard ways on to the highest

possible things—to suffer persecution for our principles, even to lay down our lives for them—and we
must be prepared to do so.

4. The Valiant Woman

A model we have here as in all such situations—
Our Blessed Lady herself. But let us understand
how, for no person was ever so little understood as
Our Blessed Lady. As already stated, we are far too
much inclined to think of her as just a sweet, amiable
sort of person, possessing indeed incredible sweetness
and beauty, gentleness and love, and all such winning characteristics. But make no mistake about it,
Our Lady was very much more than that. Of all
women, of all men, she was the strongest. She was
"the strong Woman." The Mary of the Gospel was
no shrinking miss; and if all our reading has given
us that impression of her, then we are very grievously
astray. The whole character of Our Lady was a character of strength. She was the Tower of David. She
was the Tower of Ivory. She was the Army set in
array. Do not let us misunderstand her.

Now, what was the characteristic of her whole life?
I would say respectfully, that she lived throughout
under the shadow of intolerable and ever-present
anguishing fear, a fear which reached down into her
very marrow, and rendered every single second of
her life one of inutterable torture. That dreadful

instinct of fear was certainly with her from the time of the prophecy of Simeon. We must remember that of all people she was the most versed in the prophecies of the Old Testament. Moreover, with her clearer and keener intellect she saw these things in a way that no other person could see them. Therefore, she understood all the horrors that were awaiting her Son, and of course everything that He suffered she was to suffer. Her compassion meant her Son and herself suffering together, almost in the one flesh— two people nailed to the one Cross in the end. That meant agony surpassing comprehension. All the sufferings of the world put together were as nothing compared to hers. The thought of all that the future held in store was ever present to her. In proportion to that clearness of vision and to her unparalleled strength and courage, she must have felt the weight of fear to an awful degree. Could it ever relax its torturing grip on her Immaculate Heart? Yet, from the outset, unshakingly and imperturbably she goes ahead. Never does she falter either in her step or in her look or in her soul. Yet, in her is no admixture of hardness or truculence, or of resisting for the mere sake of resisting—all of which things would be contrary to charity.

Such is our model. So, when we find that the same icy hand of fear pushes into our life and tries to press us back from duty, we should turn our thoughts to her. Thereby we do two efficacious things. Thinking with Mary, we see our duty ultra-clear; thinking of her, we challenge fear in the arena of our minds, and that challenge is half the victory. But more than that, Mary is the Mother of our souls; in her gift are the graces that will enable us to crush down that fear and manfully to march the path of duty, lead where it will on to the realization of our destiny in Christ—even on to a Cross!

VIII. UNAPOSTOLIC CATHOLICISM
AN ANOMALY

I SUPPOSE EVERYBODY, when reading the newspapers during these last momentous years, has been struck by the relatively small part the Catholic Church is playing in relation to the great disruptive happenings which are shaking the whole world. The Holy Father has been making his broken-hearted appeals in the interests of peace, but truly he may be described as "a voice crying in the wilderness," because no one seems to be listening. The Church has been just quietly elbowed to one side. That is a very perplexing thought, but it should be much more than that to us; it should be a galvanic thought, because we know that something must be wrong when such a state of things can be. And if something is wrong, then something must be done about it.

That well-known French writer, Père Plus, has defined a Christian as one to whose care has been committed his fellow-man. That signifies that every Christian has a duty—*every* Christian. Pius XI said that Catholic Action is an elementary Christian duty imposed on each person by the Sacraments of Baptism and Confirmation. And St. John Chrysostom warns us to this effect:

> "Christians, remember that at the hour of Judgment you must render an account, not for your own souls alone, but for the souls of all men."

The foregoing quotations express a truth, and that truth is this—the apostolate represents no more than normal Catholic life. The apostolic life is not a unique life, and it is not an heroic life; it is common Catholicity as God intended it and as the Church sees it—nothing more. And, if people looking on at it should acclaim it as heroic, that only means that their standards have sunk very low indeed, and that the true standard of living as expressed by those great authorities whom I have been quoting is not understood. This fact, therefore, stands forth: as the lay apostolate is only common Catholicity, all Catholics, and not merely the pick of them, are bound to be in its ranks.

This truth will help those engaged in apostolic work to take a correct view of their own position. They must not assume that in being apostles they have achieved a very special attitude, that they have climbed the spiritual peaks. The fact is that they have only established themselves in the necessary elements of Catholic duty as understood by the Church; they are really only at the ground level, and their climb has yet to begin. They must brace themselves for that climb, to the achievement of heroism. I say it again: they are only on the ground level at present. The climb is before them.

When we reflect on the heroism shown by so many during the war, the thought suggests itself: "Why should that heroic spirit be in plain evidence amongst us only when evoked by some sort of national crisis?" Note that it is not a religious crisis which evoked that heroism, but a national one. Why should we show ourselves in the full light of our possibilities only when death and danger come along to bring the element of reality into everyday life? Is it not possible for sensible people to face realities without that special stimulus? Why should we realize the fleeting character of this life and the futility of the things of this world only when imminent danger confronts us, when some national or social or emotional convulsion plants us right up against final things, and thus brings us to our senses? I think that, if we were able to live always on this level which dire happenings have set us on—if we could stabilize that sublime indifference to life and comfort, and throw that spirit into our ordinary life and work—we could simply tear asunder the existing faulty standards of the world, and in their place set up entirely new standards appropriate to the Catholic Church. Those worthy standards would call down the Omnipotence of God and force Him—very willingly, needless to say—to give us whatever we may want; to give us the conversions we want—the mass-conversions; to give us miracles of every description, and thus to shock the cynical world into looking fixedly at the Catholic Church and listening to her message.

1. Why Are There So Few Miracles To-Day?

When I talk in this way about the miraculous, the question may be asked: "Well, what do we want with miracles?" My reply is this: the Catholic Church is the carrying on of the life of Our Lord in its every aspect, and a most prominent feature of Our Lord's life was its miracles. He worked miracles as part of His ordinary mission; He spoke of them as the attendant of faith. They represented His chief way of awakening people, of attracting their eyes to Himself and shattering them out of their indifference and worldliness and making them listen to Him, follow Him, believe in Him. There is just as much necessity to-day for that sort of dazzling doctrine as there was when Our Lord was living. In fact, there is more, because we live to-day in a blasé world—a world that pays no attention to mere talking, that cannot be stirred out of its indifference by any force that is less than dynamic, a world in which such a state of affairs has arisen that any apostolic organization (where it is not despised or disregarded) is looked upon as truly heroic. I have already insisted that such a conception of the apostolate is not correct.

I stress this question of miracles, because they are desirable; they are needed. They are the supreme challenge to unbelief. They are the endorsement of our Faith, shown as such in history, shown as such in the New Testament. The preparation for the Church was miraculous; the establishment of the Church was miraculous; the spread of the Church was miraculous. It was all miraculous. And, having regard to the fact that the Church merely carries on Our Lord's life, the miraculous should be part and parcel of the mission of the Church, practically part and parcel of its everyday work. By the miraculous I do not necessarily mean (nor do I exclude either) the moving of mountains, or the raising of the dead, or the stilling of the tempest. I say I do not exclude these, for they are possible and just as desirable now as ever they were—and the Arm of God has not shortened. But I particularly mean the stilling of the tempest of problems and passions, the raising of the morally dead, the moving away of the mountains of unbelief. These are all things that we know are just as possible to-day as ever they were in the history of the Church. And yet they are not being realized! Why? Because our Catholicism has not sufficient body in it; it is only a shadow of what it is supposed to be. Even they who represent a sort of upper stratum in the flock have intolerably low standards; they are prepared to rejoice and be content when merely modest results come along, instead of having at all times a heart for the impossible. For that word "impossible" is only a human relation. With God no word shall be impossible, and to us things will range from the impossible to the possible exactly in the measure that we enlist the grace of God in our service. If we can call fully on that grace, then all things whatsoever are within our grasp. There is no problem we cannot solve, no person we cannot convert, no community we cannot win over to the Faith. There is nothing we cannot accomplish if we can but call upon the Omnipotence of God to help us. If it is objected that I seem to suggest that, as things are, we cannot count on that Omnipotence, and it is asked, "Why not?" my answer is that we do not go about the business of claiming it in the right way; our faith is low and poor and weak. Let us venture to give a little examination to that problem.

2. Miracles a Corollary of True Faith

What is wrong with the quality of our faith and conduct that we do not get the results which were forthcoming in the earlier days of the Church? When we read in the Gospel about having the faith

113

of God, the faith that moves mountains, what exactly is meant? Does it mean just a pious belief in God and in His power to do all things? With all respect I say it means nothing of the kind, because that sort of faith is possessed by even the most easy-going and thoughtless in the Catholic world. But none of such people are working the type of miracle in question. The faith that is meant must be of an entirely different quality from that which is our common possession, and which goes no farther than what I have already described as a pious belief. The faith that is wanted, the real faith, does not mean an empty sentiment, but an action. It very definitely means action—seeing God and souls, and hardly seeing anything else; then pursuing those ends with absolute determination, with complete forgetfulness of oneself, of one's own interest and one's own safety; prepared to press after these ends even if one's own destruction be entailed.

One may say this is a very extreme conception; one may ask: "Does it literally mean that I must be prepared to lay down my life, or be destroyed or ruined in some way or another in the search for the interests of God?"

My answer is that it certainly does. It is true that a much less noble degree of faith will save us. But it is not going to move away the mountains of the difficult and the impossible and to enlist in our behalf the Omnipotence of God.

Now, the faith which I describe is the kind that is required to face the gigantic and grim problems of the day; and, difficult to nature though it seems, it is by no means an impossible or unknown degree of faith, for I have seen many individuals in the ranks of the lay apostolate facing up to situations in that very spirit. I have known a fair number of cases where in the course of their work the lay apostles came to a point at which they had to decide either to stop or go on. The going on apparently meant their personal ruin. The stopping meant the abandonment of a prime work for souls to which they had committed themselves. I am happy to be able to say that in all the cases I have in mind those apostles pressed on —I do not say they did it undauntedly, but I do say they pressed on. And what was the sequel? Well, amazing to say, in every one of those cases they gained their objective completely. Surely, for those people it was a setting of their feet upon the waters and walking! Reflecting on those happenings, and making more than due allowance for coincidence, one could not but be convinced that a regular law was operating whereby the miraculous stepped in at the point where human effort and goodwill had done their utmost—they could do no more, they could but cast themselves appealingly on the Omnipotent. We do not realize that the miraculous is, as it were, on tap for us like that. We get the idea from what we have read or heard that the miraculous is something altogether out of the way, something unexplainable in its incidence, subject to no law, experienced only at specially designated places like Lourdes; we regard miraculous interventions as manifestations of God's singular predilection for special souls, but certainly something not to be realized by common people like ourselves. That is a complete error. From my experience, such as it has been, I would say that the miraculous in its different grades is absolutely on tap for anybody that requires it, and is prepared to pay the price.

3. Confusing the Natural and Supernatural

I am inclined to fear that the ordinary faith which is current even in estimable Catholic communities, is more natural than supernatural. Herein, I seem to be voicing a contradiction: faith being supernatural, how can it be natural? What I mean is that we may use a supernatural power after a natural fashion, which almost amounts to not using it at all. As a parallel, consider the case of a bird which has powerful wings, and yet is satisfied to walk the ground like the common hen—or worse still, to waddle along like the duck. Our faith, like that bird, is meant to fly and reach the higher region, but it does not fly.

It keeps to "the level and the low," and walks the ground like the hen or duck.

Such a use of faith means that nothing is attempted unless it can be justified from the natural angle as well as from the supernatural. Then, when we run up against an obstacle, instead of seeking to fly over it by the miraculous powers of grace, we allow it to bring us to a complete standstill. We regard the natural difficulty as final. We do not exactly rule faith out, but we harness it and subject it to natural considerations. The result of that conception of faith has been disastrous. Do Catholic communities emerge in bold relief from among others by their mode of life and by their standards? Sometimes it is not easy to distinguish them. How often have we to take refuge in saying: "Oh yes, we may not ostensibly be living different lives, but we have the Faith!" That is a mighty poor defense. Yet, too often it is the best that can be made. Look, for instance, at the Continent of Europe—in previous ages the fount of Catholicity, the furnisher of missionaries, the nursery of Saints. To-day, Europe in the Gospel phrase "walks no more with Christ," does not want to walk any more with Him, and appears impossible of conversion. And we, shackled by our weakness of faith, stand looking helplessly on!

Again, so dominating is that merely natural attitude of Catholics towards their faith and the powers

of their religion that there is considerable danger
—which has to a large extent become an actuality—
that we may regard the Church as being limited in
her activities, in her possibilities, and in her accom-
plishments, as any ordinary earthly institution is limited. In practice we assume that what an ordinary
institution can do, the Catholic Church can do, and
what an ordinary worldly institution cannot do, the
Catholic Church cannot do. Is this statement of the
situation an exaggeration? Well, read the papers
and see. Or ponder our own conversations and judge
if we have not erred into that line of thought. I
give you an example. No doubt you have noticed
the consoling articles which have appeared of late in
the Catholic Press of some country proving that
in the year 1987 or so the Catholic Church will have
a larger membership than all other religions. Why?
It is because the Catholic birth-rate is higher than
any other in such country. You see, it is by the birth-
rate and the ordinary law of multiplication alone that
we are going to have more Catholics in such and such
a year! I ask you if that is not looking on the Catholic Church as a purely human institution? I do not
mean to say that God does not use that way of adding
souls to His Church. But is He thus limited? Did
God ever intend the increase of His Church to depend on the marriage-rate and the birth-rate only?
You know that the very suggestion is ridiculous.

We boast that, since birth control is more prevalent in non-Catholic communities than in ours, our numbers will therefore eventually predominate. But what about the loss of souls in the long interval of waiting while our numbers grow? Is there to be no question of the conversion of men by direct attack? What about the days when Ireland sent its missionaries out over Europe? For what? It was to convert men, to convert masses of men. Are these days altogether gone? Yes, under present conditions of faith they almost appear to be. Think of the conversion of England as it was once accomplished. Could it be won to the Faith once more as was done in those early days? Again I suggest, not under present conditions. Numerically Catholics are not going ahead there at all. For the 10,000 or so conversions a year are counterbalanced by the leakage. In all the newspaper surveys of the Catholic position, I have not seen a word about the miraculous converting power of the Church. And what of the greater problem of converting France—and the still more difficult one of converting Russia?

With the persistence of this wholly natural attitude we work largely on natural lines. The idea of getting miraculous help from God is absent. If we get impatient at the idea of tedious extension through the birth-rate, and aim at direct conversions, then again our planning follows purely human lines. How often have we heard something of this kind: "The future lies in our getting hold of the children. We cannot spend time on the adults because they are hopeless." And the attempted conversion of a country resolves itself to this, that we endeavor to educate the children and we leave the adults practically alone. We have little idea of looking as of old for mass-conversions of men, no idea of forcing—by a faith that does not stagger—the Omnipotence of God to sweep down and gather whole continents into His Church. Our thinking is done along natural lines. Even the choicest types of our people are inclined thus to let the natural dictate to the supernatural. Even the best of us are incapable of judging these things, and there is great danger in applying our own opinions to some situation wherein the decision rests with God. What is naturally eligible and likely-looking is not necessarily the same in the supernatural order.

4. *An Unfortunate Mode of Thought*

Now, let us offer an example, absolutely typical of the experience of ourselves and of everybody else, illustrating unfortunately our ordinary mode of thought. An influential and good Catholic, in a position to give employment, was approached recently about a girl and asked to give her a chance in a job. This girl had been misconducting herself some time before, and the fact was mentioned. The reply to the request was that the only remedy for anyone of that type was to lock her up permanently in an institution. Study that sweeping assertion with its implication, and you are shocked to find that it reduces the divinely guided Church precisely to the level of the ordinary prison system. It suggests that the Church, like the prison system, is unable to secure a conversion other than by locking up the person sought to be converted. I feel that every Catholic heart will instinctively repudiate that suggestion as utterly intolerable, a gospel of hopelessness.

Yet, do we not usually fetter by worldly reasonings the illimitable powers of faith? So long as there is dry land, we are prepared to walk the rough road that leads to souls. But the moment that land ends and the waters begin, is there one amongst us that will set his feet upon those waters and go on, though he knows that a soul is the price of his doing so? Rather will he not weigh himself and that soul in the balance, and nearly always it will be his side that goes down and his own interests that will win the day. Is it strange, then, that we are not able to call upon the Omnipotence of God in our various works? Do not take me as suggesting that we are not ever calling upon and obtaining graces from God. Manifestly we are, but we are not drawing upon His *Omnipotence*—by which I mean His capacity to do what is impossible to nature (including the splendidly miraculous). Yet, in the greatness of our ambitions and our efforts we should aim at nothing less than the impossible. The result would be veiled miracles—batches of people capitulating and being converted, big unsolved problems being readily solved.

I am satisfied that such miracles are available for any who resolutely reach for them. But that word "resolutely" is the difficulty. If you want them, you must act, and act with faith-centered determination. Remember this: our religion, if it is to accomplish anything, must be supernatural. That means it must break to an extent with the purely natural. It will in consequence pay scant attention to the claims of worldly prudence. Heroic faith represents the application of the rules of God, and *only the rules of God*, to your work and your everyday life—the unwavering, unconditional application of His rules. I repeat that you must break with the natural, for if you try to balance one foot on the natural and the other on the supernatural, you will in practice believe that it is the natural that supports you and not the supernatural. So believing, you may ask, but it shall not be given you; you may knock, and it shall not be opened to you!

IX. MARRIAGE—AT A PRICE!

ACTIVE CATHOLICS should be happy in each other's company. Friendships should form—man with man, girl with girl, man with girl. These friendships should be superior to common friendships, because in them there is an additional element—the spiritual. They grow in a supernatural soil instead of in a merely natural one. Very often, too, they are germinated in that soil. The effect of this alliance of the natural and supernatural principles should be to knit soul to soul—almost to fuse them. Wherefore, every "Catholic Action friendship" should express a special intensity and nobility: it should be like unto the love of David and Jonathan—if it be not as that of Darby and Joan!

An interesting development of Catholic Action has been its marriages. There have already been many of them; others are incubating—marriages between Legionaries, Jocists, and so on. We should be rejoiced by this manifestation, and intrigued by its possibilities to Catholic Action, to the world and to religion.

Prima facie, such unions should be successful. If ever the basic ingredients of success are to be present, surely it will be in a marriage between young Catholic apostles! Nature and grace combine harmoniously to this end. In the first place, you have two right-intentioned, seriously minded, self-sacrificing, tender-hearted, self-reliant people—a real man and a real woman.

In the second place, you have these two souls entering on their life's partnership in quite a special way under the auspices of the Most Blessed Virgin. "I am all thine, My Queen, My Mother," they must often have repeated with their lips and meant with their hearts. They have given their little leisure, and the best that is in them, in active service of her. In their future life she will be to them, no less than in the past, a regal queen and a solicitous mother. In addition, she will exercise in their regard a new influence, a matrimonial rôle. For in the measure that each belongs to her, so will they belong to each other. Thus, dependence on her, which ought to character-ize every lay apostle, will constitute an additional, potent principle of oneness between them.

What, indeed, may one not suppose of such a union —quickened, nurtured, as it is in the bosom of the Mother of Divine Grace? Surely not less than that it be a very model of marriage?

Therefore, these marriages of young apostles are to be welcomed, May there be more and more of them, undertaken with ever-ascending standards, and destined to draw in their train a new order!

To bring a new order to pass, two conditions must be fulfilled. The first is that the standards of those marriages must be far higher than current ones, so that they will challenge and then captivate the imagination, and in time be adopted by all the worthier elements in the community.

The second requirement is that these marriages be in large number. One swallow does not make a summer. One lone soldier does not win a war. Neither does one ideal marriage—nor even several of them —create a new model of marriage.

1. "We Cannot Get Married Yet"

This second requirement is not being fulfilled; therefore, the first one cannot be operative. "Catholic Action marriages" are not yet taking place in sufficient number to form a new pattern. Around us we see many minded to marry, but hesitating. Hesitating at what?

Hesitating at an intimidatory array of obstacles. With telegraphic economy of words, a daily newspaper has stated the position: "Boss says 'no rise'; Corporation says 'no houses'; landlady says 'no babies'; grocer says 'no tick'."[1] Funny, but only on the surface. Undoubtedly the dice are loaded against

[1] "No tick" is colloquial for "No credit!"

those wishful to marry—so much so that according to the safety-first mentality of the day most men would be mad to marry.

The crucial difficulty is that of finance: "No money to get married! Next year!" And after that another and another year. Many next years! The years of youth are let slip away while waiting for that stage of sufficient money—for that tide which never rises high enough to let the ship away. But the ship is meant to sail—that is, marriage is meant for most men. The moral is plain: the ship must be lightened; the standards of marriage must be mended.

What is "enough money"? A girl defined it for me recently. (Let me explain that I was not proposing to her.) She put it at 3,000 dollars per annum! But that is ruling out the institution of marriage altogether. Therefore, we must set the figure lower— much lower.

How much lower? Let us proceed to the opposite extreme. What about the weekly sum which your country (whichever one it is) has fixed as its maintenance allowance for the unemployed man with a wife. You laugh; you do not take me seriously. But people are getting married on it. Do not take me as urging that it ought to be done; but actually it is being done. Suppose that we concede that it is inadequate to marry on. Then how much higher are we to go, while still keeping *far* below that absurd 3,000 dollars?

Here someone will object: "It is impossible to fix an arbitrary figure. Every person's level will be different. Many circumstances have to be taken into account, including that of social position."

How smooth and round is this objection! It looks so reasonable and it is so wrong. It is justified to the extent that one cannot think in terms of a definite marrying figure. And no doubt, individual circumstances, including social standing, have *some* bearing. But the full import of the objection is that every young pair are entitled to start off on the level where they would like to be, or where their parents left off. That rule would sabotage marriage. Here is a better one: "Marry on less than what you think to be necessary." This is almost the opposite of the other. But analyse it and you will find that it is psychologically sound and in line with reality.

No standards are right which would have the effect of making marriage a privileged preserve, or of narrowing it down to a smaller category than the general run of mankind. For marriage is divinely intended to be the ordinary human relation. Is not, therefore, the man who is getting common wages, and yet refrains from marriage on the grounds of "not enough," setting up a standard for himself which is higher than that intended by God?

Many will protest that they are only waiting till they are a little better off. But when is that going to be? You are on a fixed wage which will only go up when a strike forces it up; and that strike will itself have been forced by, and will probably lead to, a rise in the cost of living, leaving no one any better off when the vicious circle has been completed. .

"But no," you correct me, "a few years will find me better-placed. I get an annual increment—*or* I am next in line of succession for my boss's shoes."

That few years may be ten. They may be more, and they are the building, vital years; so that yours may be a middle-aged marriage, one with the enthusiasm gone out of it, a "comfort marriage," perhaps a childless one.

So, if you are not likely to be any better off by waiting; or if you are only going to be better off by a big stroke of luck (which does happen occasionally, but not to you and me!); or if you are sure to be better off only when your youth (and what is worse, your future wife's youth) has waned, then, is it wise, even from the human standpoint, to wait?

2. *Getting Married for God*

Why not lean on God, instead of on human considerations solely? He will work a little miracle for you—or a big one—if you but make a solid act of faith in Him; which means taking the step that is not clear to you. You desire to embark on what is popularly called the sea of matrimony, but there is no boat. So, trust God to sustain you, set your foot on the water, and walk. You must not hope for an unaided miracle.

Chorus of indignation: "A reckless, improvident marriage! You condemn these young people to a life of hardship!"

Perhaps so, and what of it? Are not other young people being stimulated to enter monasteries, go on the Missions, essay the heroic but unprofitable things of life for the sake of high ideal?

It is retorted: "But marriage is different. One gets married for happiness."

True, and I might add: to escape from "digs," from the drudgery of office or counter, for independence, for improvement of position—or out of infatuation. In a word, for self and nothing else!

Do people ever think of getting married for God? Is there any reality in the phrase, "vocation of marriage"? Or is this expression no more than lip-service? A set of ideas quite different from true vocational ideals governs the general approach to marriage.

It is not that people do not try to lead holy lives in matrimony. Of course, they do. But the butcher, the baker, the candlestick-maker—and the civil servant—also try to lead holy lives. But that does not by itself constitute those occupations vocations except in the conventional sense of the word. As you objected a moment ago (but in a contrary sense), marriage is different. It is a true vocation in every sense of the word, because it is a sacramental state—like the priesthood itself. Therefore, marriage is an immense thing, elevated farther above merely occupational states than Mount Everest is reared above ground level.

But for full efficacy vocations and Sacraments require coöperation; and in regard to the great Sacrament of Matrimony this condition is not being sufficiently satisfied. Its big moment is esteemed to be the wedding ceremony; after that there is little or no advertence to the fact of a sacramental condition. If graces flow, it is because God freely gives them, rather than because of any effort to earn them. For in the everyday marriage the main factors are not faith, hope and charity, but pounds, shillings and pence; not holiness but worldly pursuits; not God but sheer self!

Being a sacramental state, the graces potential in Matrimony must simply be unlimited, transforming, ready to seize on every circumstance and to fill every moment of life. But, without the vocational idea and the advertence, those wonder-working graces will largely be unreaped. This is the reason for all those unhappy or commonplace unions—indistinguishable from the marriages of other creeds—which surround us.

Now, here is my proposition to young Catholic apostles. Why not marry in the full spirit of vocation —with the intention of deliberately exploiting the spirtual gold-mine of Matrimony . . . in such fashion that the ideals and devotedness of John, who gets married, are not inferior to those of his brother James who becomes a Cistercian, or of his sister Nellie who enters Carmel?

Why should the Religious vocation be conceived in terms of renunciation and unadorned living, whereas the marriage ambition is the opposite? In marriage we moderns only renounce or live simply to the extent that we are constrained thereto by financial pressure. How big a house can we afford—instead of how few rooms can we manage with? How much can we put into those rooms—instead of the Religious ideal: how little can we do with?

Not only do we view marriage and enter on it with incorrect standards and emptiness of ideal, but we carry on through married life in the same non-spiritual track—"with proud eye and insatiable heart," as the Psalmist says. Nothing fills our longing. Each rung higher on the ladder of good fortune, instead of gratifying existing wants, only opens a wider horizon for them. Up go our standards, so that often we are worse off than we were before. New home, new furniture, new friends, new schools for the children, new style of living! But the same old will-o'-the-wisp remains, leading us on, enticing us off the road—into debt or some other morass. Where is the vocational, sacramental point of view in all this?

3. Demonstrating the Ideal of Marriage

So back to the charge again I come and say: "Who among you will lend yourselves to the Lord to afford to the world a practical demonstration of true marriage—not crawling in the dust, earthy, but winged for heaven, a sacramental state, a vocation?" As Browning says:

"Those who live as models for the mass,
Are singly of more value than they all."

Marriage is God's plan for carrying on the world, which means that it is our normal spiritual formation. In the main, He intends each man (and woman) to cleave to some one woman (one man) so that they will help each other—soul and body—in the painful pilgrimage of life, which it is not good for man to make alone. Furthermore, He wants them to increase and multiply so that earth—and later heaven —will be peopled with souls.

But present-day standards frustrate this design. They tend to put marriage out of bounds for many men and to debase it for the remainder. Necessarily those standards are wrong, anti-social, anti-God.

How correct them? There is only the one way. It is to hold up to the eye of the world a true model of marriage, that is marriage undertaken in conscious cooperation with God, in the intention, spirit and actuality of vocation. This must be a practical model; that is, not one devoted pair, but many, must exhibit it. Moreover, if it is to challenge the perverted standards, it must afford dramatic lessons of holiness, renunciation, simple living, even to the degree of hardship.

Again the critics' chorus resounds: "Poverty! misery! unhappiness!"

I retort: "Do not so unthinkingly cry 'poverty' or 'misery,' for thereby you seem to say that God and mammon must be served together. And as for what you call 'unhappiness,' do not confound true happiness (which *is* found in vocation, holiness, self-sacrifice) with what is nothing but a counterfeit, namely, mere pleasure-sipping and jollification."

A writer in the *Catholic Digest* of May, 1940, declares:

"The Creator cares very little about human glee. He wants growth. He has an earth to people and a plan to perfect. You don't buy happiness while you are working towards ends like glee. You buy trouble and rebellion, growing pains, and a whale of a beating."

Colorful language! Yes, but an answer to those who believe that we live but to make merry.

Those who try to fashion this new model of marriage will need to lead sacrificial lives. But those who thus lay down their lives, shall save them—and many others with their own. Their faith shall free God's hands for munificent giving. Incidentally, He will furnish them with all that is needful to them— including the proper and priceless gift of marriage, a love that will combine two souls in one, two hearts into one heart. He says:

"No man can serve two masters; for either he will hate the one and love the other, or else he will sustain the one and despise the other. You cannot serve God and mammon.

"Therefore I say to you, be not solicitous for your life, what you shall eat; nor yet for your body, what you shall put on. Is not the life more than the meat, and the body than the raiment? Behold the birds of the air; they neither sow, nor do they reap, nor gather into barns; and your Heavenly Father feedeth them. Are not you of much more value than they? And which of you by taking thought can add to his stature a single cubit?

"And for raiment, why are you solicitous? Consider the lilies of the field, how they grow; they labor not, nor do they spin. Yet, I say to you that not even Solomon in all his glory was arrayed as one of these. But if God doth so clothe the grass of the field, which is to-day and to-morrow is cast into the oven, how much more you, O ye of little faith!

"Be not solicitous, therefore, saying, 'What shall we eat?' or 'What shall we drink?' or 'Wherewith shall we be clothed?' (for after all these things the heathens seek); for your Father knoweth that you have need of all these things. Seek ye, therefore, first the kingdom of God and His justice, and all these things shall be added unto you" (Matthew, vi. 24-33).

"Reckless! Improvident!" No, you cannot say that to Providence Himself. You must take Providence at His word. Faith is taking Providence at His word. Why leave marriage out of the things that this is to be applied to?

But I am not suggesting that everyone should rush headlong into matrimony. Nor am I echoing those married men who (like the fox that had lost its tail) want by various means to force all single men into marriage—as if they were jealous of them.

In fact, I do not address those who do not want to get married, but only those who are anxious to, or who are thinking of it. Though here I venture on a word of warning to the others—that those who are refraining from marriage for purely selfish motives

135

will probably find their days bleak and lonely enough when the autumn or fall of life comes on them.

Within the ranks of young enthusiastic active Catholics there are very many who have the capacity, and the dormant will, to make this venture in faith. Each pair who do so will find imitators. Many imitators will make a new school of thought. Obviously, a new school of thought on this subject would mean a changed world. The time is over-ripe for the attempt. For even in its lower aspect, as a human institution, marriage is in peril.

X. MARKS OF THE APOSTOLATE

THERE CAN BE no doubt at all in the mind of an instructed Christian that he has a real duty to be an apostle amongst his fellows. It is a duty that flows from the very nature of the Church as the Mystical Body of Christ, a duty dictated by the love of God and of our neighbor, a duty resultant upon the reception of the Sacraments of Baptism and Confirmation, a duty of obedience to the Vicars of Christ, a duty even of patriotism. That every Christion should acquit himself nobly of that duty is the greatest need, not only of the Church, but of the world to-day. Hence, it will be regarded by Satan as his greatest work to prevent the apostolic idea effectively permeating the Church.

It is important that the priest should be given his rightful place in any apostolic movement. There has been in some places a notable tendency in the opposite direction, a tendency to refuse to the priest the position that is absolutely necessary for him if he is to form and direct those who, in their apostolic work, are simply the extension of himself. The success of the apostolate will be judged entirely according to the spiritual quality developed in the apostles and brought by them to bear on their work. It is precisely the development of spiritual quality that is the work of the priest, who must, therefore, be the mainspring of the whole movement. Far better, I think, to allow the priest too large a part than unduly to restrict his influence.

1. Is Knowledge Indispensable?

Again, the true notion of the apostolate must at all costs be preserved. Père Plus has defined it as "radiating Christ," a definition that is exact and comprehensive. The spreading of religious knowledge is only part—and not the most important part—of the apostolate; far more important are incitement to good, the expounding of quite elementary facts, and the imparting of conviction. The substance of the apostolate is within the capacity of even the subnormal man.

The cardinal principle, "Every man an apostle," must never be in jeopardy. If you think of the apostolate as the spread of religious knowledge, that principle is immediately imperiled, because before you will allow one to undertake apostolic work, you must logically demand some kind of qualification by way of knowledge. The result is the limiting of the numbers of potential apostles.

The Pope has said that the first apostles of working men ought to be themselves working men. Obviously, these working-men apostles will not need the same amount of knowledge as a barrister carrying on an apostolate amongst his friends at law. He is dealing with men of roughly the same intelligence as himself; he can talk to them about politics, about war, about sport. Then why should he not talk to them about religion? Why need he study to do so? Failure to understand this very important point is one reason why an immense number of potential apostles are never called upon by those officially in charge of Catholic Action.

We have suggested that the amount of knowledge possessed by the average Catholic working man is far more than that usually accredited to him. He has been attending church, reading his prayer book and hearing sermons for perhaps forty or fifty years; he has been reading the Catholic press regularly; he has attended his Catholic club and joined in informal discussions with his companions—surely after all this he knows enough about religion in general and his own Faith in particular to carry on an effective apostolate amongst his fellow-workmen? An even more important point is this: that man, and he is legion, has in his heart a living, vivid picture of his Faith, of something that means more to him than anything else upon earth. All he lacks is the encouragement, the organization which will make him use the capacity he possesses to put it over.

It is a matter of common experience that knowledge is very often a positive obstacle to apostolic action. It seems to set up a psychological barrier between the apostle and the one upon whom he is trying to exert his influence; it somehow submerges the more intimate and natural approach, and seems to set up a gulf between two otherwise similar souls. We heard the other day of a clergyman of the Established Church who had always been attracted towards Catholicism, but felt that he could not accept the doctrine of the Real Presence. He studied everything he could find on the subject, but faith still eluded him. He knew the Catholic theology of the Eucharist almost backwards—but all, apparently, to no purpose. Then, he chanced to be out in the country with his car, and called at a cottage for some water. The woman there mistook him for a Catholic priest; he explained who he was, adding that he wanted to become a Catholic, but found difficulty in accepting the dogma of the Blessed Sacrament. That simple woman brought him into the little room, sat him down by the fire, and in simple language explained just what the Holy Eucharist meant to her. The minister, now a priest, said afterwards that that simple explanation, delivered with real conviction, was responsible for his conversion, in spite of the fact that he had previously held long discussions with some of the greatest theologians of the Catholic Church.

I am daily more convinced that what is needed to-day is not so much argument as the simple presentation of the great truths of faith in an appealing form. The technique of the look-around store must be adopted; our goods must be displayed as attractively as possible so as to make them acceptable. But, at the same time, nothing will be gained, and a great deal lost, by a policy of watering down Catholic teaching to suit Protestant or other prejudices. The Catholic has something of which one outside the Church would rightly be jealous, if only he were aware of its value. The task of the apostle is precisely to impart to that soul such awareness. The last way to do that is by argument; the first by an approach that breathes humility, affection, and sincerity.

From another point of view, there is so little of genuine intellectual Christianity left in the English-speaking world—apart from such places as Eire—that we must steadily approach nearer and nearer the technique of the foreign missions. The convinced Christian and the man-in-the-street of the present day are becoming less and less able to discuss together any of the great questions of the moment which have a moral or religious bearing, simply because there is no common basis upon which they can base their discussion. Take, for example, marriage.

For the good pagan the approach is usually utilitarian, often selfish, and always oblivious of the divine institution and sacred nature of matrimony. The Christian regards marriage in such an utterly different light that any real discussion is bound to be at cross-purposes. Certainly the Catholic apostle will benefit little by advanced knowledge on the subject, because it is the simple exposition of merely elementary facts that is required.

Study is good in itself. Viewed purely from the standpoint of the lay apostleship, it remains good so long as it is undertaken with a view to action, and is not allowed to impede or supplant that action in any way. Unfortunately, too many embark upon a course of study with a view to preparing themselves for action but never progress so far. They realize how little they really know, and so study more and more. They become more and more convinced that they can never know sufficient; they begin to unearth abstruse difficulties about which they had never heard before—and the result is complete inaction, and the reduction to absurdity of that vital principle, "Every man an apostle." Once more the devil is triumphant; his cunning has succeeded; the army opposed to him has lost another recruit. Yes, everything that would limit the number of potential apostles to a few, an ineffective minority, must be a lie, because it is a denial in practice of a principle that is certainly true, namely, that every Christian is bound to be an apostle.

Since writing the above, we have come across the following, which summarizes exactly the point at issue: [1]

"The primary purpose of Catholic Action is to carry forth into the world the power of a God-filled personality—*organum pulsatum a Spiritu sancto*. . . .

"The apostolate of reason is always a necessity; there is always need of those who can explain and defend the Faith, and state it again in terms which can be understood by the contemporary mind; indeed it may be that now, more than ever before, this necessity weighs upon us. And yet perhaps it is not the supreme task of to-day. The world gets very tired of argument. It would be more accurate to say that the labors of reason *alone* are not the supreme task; and that the world gets very tired of argument which it feels to spring only from the head. . . .

"The supreme task of to-day is a question of being; because it is a question of bringing back to the world the direct *experience* of the power of love in the world; it is a question of bringing it face to face with the immensity of the Paraclete, *the Strengthener*, filling and shining through the bodies of men. When you have been shaken to the roots of your being by the mere presence of some-

[1] "The Divine Pity," by Fr. G. Vann, O.P., p. 59.

one who stands for a truth, then you are impelled to examine the truth he stands for, and predisposed to apprehend it. 'Kindle within them the *fire* of Thy love,' then 'they shall be re-created and Thou shalt renew the face of the earth.' "

There is a belief prevalent that the direct approach to souls is impossible. Every kind of pretext is used to avoid it, and thus the fear about which we have already written a great deal is given full rein. Moreover, such action as there is always remains in the preparatory stage, and never really gets to grips with souls. The most important element of the apostolate —the diffusion of the religious system of the Church —takes second place to such things as the social question.

Consider the following. The apostolate is by definition the radiation of Christ; but Pope Pius X has told us that the first and indispensable source of the Christian spirit is the Sacred Liturgy of the Church. Unfortunately, the meaning of that word "Liturgy" has been taken up wrongly in certain quarters, and, as Pius XII has pointed out in the Encyclical on the Mystical Body, a doubtful liturgical movement has grown up in some places. Two great faults were apparent: firstly, the depreciation of the value of private prayer, and secondly an overemphasis on externals—rubrics, vestments, chant, and so forth. The lay apostolate, while giving its due place to private prayer, must aim at diffusing a wide understanding of the inner meaning of the Mass and of all the Sacraments, and, consequently, of the full significance of the life of grace in the soul. The true source of the Christian spirit is not primarily the *words* of the Liturgy, but the life of grace imparted to the soul by assistance at Holy Mass. Therefore, it surely is obvious that the most certain way to radiate the spirit of Christ is to spread abroad a real appreciation of the religious system of the Church. That is the genuine apostolate.

2. *Personal Contact the Key to Success*

We have already stressed the importance of personal contact. It is our firm conviction that the approach to souls will be effective precisely in the degree in which it approaches the personal and departs from the general. The latter form of approach is easier, more glamorous, and offers to the superficially minded more prospect of immediate success. But the former will always pay best in the long run. Not that the mass approach is entirely useless and to be disregarded. No; the distribution of literature in an impersonal way, public lecturing, demonstrations, the radio—all these things are excellent in themselves and are to be encouraged, but they should not use up forces which would be better employed in the organization of an apostolic system based on personal contact.

Look at the life of Our Lord. The Gospels might almost be called the story of the personal contacts of Jesus with souls. He was "all things to all men," understanding all, sympathizing with all, helping all, encouraging all. By far the most of His time was spent moving about amongst the people, going from home to home, meeting them as they came out to Him in the streets and lanes. Had He so wished, He could have remained the distant orator; He could have tried to gather apostles by appealing for them in the synagogues of Capharnaum or Jerusalem. But that was not His method.

"The Kingdom of Heaven is like leaven which a woman has taken and buried away in three measures of meal, enough to leaven the whole batch." [1]

"And as He walked by the sea of Galilee, Jesus saw two brethren . . . and He said to them: 'Come and follow Me; I will make you into fishers of men.' " [2]

True, Jesus preached; but the great work of His life in which the foundation of the Church consisted was the careful choice and training of His closest followers who were to carry on His work after the Ascension. That was a hidden, personal apostolate. In

[1] Matt., xiii. 33.   [2] Matt., iv. 18.

the words of a French writer, it was the pouring of the soul of Jesus into the souls of the twelve.

Or glance at the history of the Church and the lives of the Saints, and do you not find the same truth exemplified? The colonies of monks that grew up in the desert in the very earliest days of the religious life offer us many striking examples of the value and effectiveness of the apostolate of personal contact; the case of the Founders of the great Orders is a particularly prominent example. They gathered their disciples, and their Institutes spread by this means. We might add the very notable cases, too, of the famous penitents. Was it not as if one soul poured forth the life of grace into another that had been prepared to receive it by sympathy and understanding?

Already we have pointed out the importance of approaching crowds through the individuals who compose them, for crowds are simply multiplications of immortal souls. Each of these souls is infinitely precious; each has been redeemed by the Precious Blood of Christ; each is meant to be the dwelling-place of the Eternal Trinity; each, to quote the well-known phrase of St. Charles, is diocese enough for a bishop. But no two of them are alike. In its past, in its present, in its future, each differs from every other soul; each is a problem in itself, a problem stretching throughout time into eternity. The apostle will secure results only in so far as he can approach each personally and individually.

You cannot spiritualize men in bulk; saints are not mass-produced. If conversions depended on the reaching of people in bulk by such means as the radio, the printed word, mass meetings, and so on, this age of scientific publicity should also be one of conversions on a grand scale. On the contrary, it is being found difficult even to defend the fold of Christ against the ravages of the wolf called neo-paganism. The reason is that all these means of publicity, while they may be very efficacious in worldly propaganda, lack the most essential element in the apostolate—the contact of one soul with another or, better, the outpouring of one soul into another. To the listener the radio is a voice rather than a person; literature is cold print rather than an enthusiastic soul; and the member of the crowd feels lost in the multitude around him.

Have we not experience on our side? Who has not heard the slogan: "A visiting priest makes a church-going people"? There are figures to prove that in those places in which the clergy have systematically and conscientiously carried out the house-to-house visitation of the people, the spiritual level of the people has been remarkably high; and where the clergy have failed in that duty, the level has been low. Again, in the case of many of the so-called "marriage converts," how often they appear to have the Faith before they begin their formal instructions! The non-Catholic young man has already been converted by the influence of his bride-to-be; he has come under the spell of a personality to whom the Faith means everything; he cannot do otherwise than embrace that same Faith. In many other cases we see the same thing—souls brought to the Church, not by a clear-cut appeal to the intellect, but by the influence of a truly Christian soul.

From what has been written the conclusion may have already emerged that, excellent as are the modern methods of propaganda for worldly objects, we must not make the mistake of relying on them alone when the conversion of souls is at stake, or of taking it for granted that they will be as instrumental in bringing men to Christ as they are in bringing them to a film. They ought always to be supplemented as far as possible by an organized apostolate of personal contact.

There is an important proviso. This personal contact which appears to be so necessary for the apostolate must not be any kind of contact. Indeed, contact is a most unsuitable word, for it conveys the impression merely of a touch, whereas the idea is rather that of a fusion, of the pouring out of one soul into another. In a word, it must be a contact of genuine spiritual love, which implies tact, sympathy, understanding, gentleness, sweetness, patience and, above all, humility. The ideal, of course, is to see our Divine Lord in everybody and to strive to serve Him in His members, approaching them, not as the superior approaches an inferior or even as an equal approaches an equal, but as the inferior approaches a superior, as the servant approaches his Master. Thus will the spirit of philanthrophy or mere human pity be guarded against, and the maximum spiritual effect guaranteed.

Another benefit of the personal and direct approach is that it guards against vagueness. Not only is a vague apostolate of very little value, but it is often positively harmful in the sense that it leaves the door wide open for the entry of discouragement. Individuals or organizations will labor for years in a vague way attacking what they consider to be grave evils in a community or a locality—bad conversation, a low level of entertainment, false ideas about marriage, evil literature, and the like; and when, naturally, they can see no definite results of their efforts, they lose heart and cease work altogether. I have seen it happen over and over again, particularly in the case of organizations which believe strongly in the "inquiry" method. Another evil result of this line of conduct is that, when another society starts work in the place, it will be informed either that the situation is altogether hopeless or that the work it intends to undertake has already been done.

3. Sincerity and Simplicity

Another tendency on the part of some individuals and societies is to indulge in propaganda on behalf of their own particular movement. This may be excellent; but at least they ought first to make certain that it is a movement and not a mere blue-print they are boosting. It is only too easy to draw up a fine scheme in one's mind—people with little practical experience are good at such things—and then boost it with the idea of recruiting people who will put it into operation. If the scheme is a good one and will work (and that would be quite exceptional in such a case), it would probably be wrecked because there would not be enough work in the beginning for all the recruits gained; if the scheme is not a practical one (as is usually the case), the only result attained is the unfortunate one of disheartening possibly a large number of earnest young people, and so being the cause of their taking no further part in apostolic work.

It is of vital importance that the means—the organization or system itself—should never be allowed to overshadow the purpose in view, the saving of souls. It has been known to happen that people have had such credulity in the child of their own brain that, in spite of clear proof of its ineffectiveness, they have persevered with it and at the same time ruled out other worthier and truly successful movements. Just as there is room in the Church for very many different types of Religious Orders, so there must be place for many different movements all grouped under the one heading of the lay apostolate. To exclude a movement that is known to do good work merely on the pretext that it may interfere with those already set up, often has the appearance of selfishness or pride. Each system should be judged from the supreme standpoint of its effectiveness in working for souls along the lines we have indicated throughout these pages, and that criterion should always take precedence over local pride or personal considerations.

Again, any apostolic system that is to succeed must be simple in its organization and plan of action; it is very easy, through overenthusiasm, to overorganize. Committees and sub-committees are set up; numerous officers are appointed; all kinds of contacts are made; complicated instructions are issued; various forms are printed—and the result is that the organization becomes an end in itself, and good for souls is prevented by seemingly interminable red-tape. Or a bottle-neck is formed on the pretext of coördinating all apostolic effort in a locality with the result that societies which hitherto flourished soon find themselves suffocated and frustrated to such an extent that they carry on a merely nominal existence. For many years, perhaps, they had independently carried on magnificent work; now they are told that nothing must be done without the consent of the central administration lest there be any overlapping. The result, as bitter experience has proved, is the end of that magnificent work and the loss of many excellent workers to the cause.

4. Needless Multiplication of Qualifications

Recently we have seen a notable trend towards the multiplication of prerequisites for the apostolate. One publication that happened to come our way was almost humorous in this respect. Every would-be apostle is asked to assess himself on a percentage basis in regard to the degree in which he possesses certain qualities of body or mind. The first list is given as follows: appearance, posture, neatness, cheerful expression, pleasing voice, energy. The average is to be worked out and that becomes one's "Apostolic Quotient." We have visions of Boards of Catholic Action sitting in committee to assess the "Apostolic Quotients" of their workers; even the most serious-minded person must see something humorous in such a situation. But it is a desperately serious matter, because it is hitting directly at the very principle we have been vindicating all through these pages, namely, that every Catholic must be an apostle. The more prerequisites you demand, the less apostles you will have.

Let us give another quotation: "Here is a check list for the apostle. . . .

1. Do you take a bath daily?
2. Do you keep your hair neat and clean?
3. Do you keep your face and hands clean at all times?
4. Do you wash your teeth twice a day and use a mouth-wash daily?
5. Are your clothes always neat, clean, well-pressed and mended?
6. Are your shoes shined and in repair?
7. Do you give yourself a manicure weekly?
8. Are your white (or light) collars, cuffs, etc., snowy white and spotless?
9. If you are a girl, do you use make-up excessively?
10. Are your fingers denicotinized?
11. Are your underwear and your socks and stockings fresh and clean?"

And so it goes on and on.

Imagine that examen as applied to the many hundreds of the most successful workers of the Legion of Mary in Dublin! The idea is simply ludicrous. It is far more important to insist on all undertaking apostolic work under proper direction; all the details mentioned above will then take care of themselves.

To obscure the vital principle—*every* Catholic an apostle—is playing into the devil's hands.

Let me repeat. The greatest need of the Church to-day is to impress upon all its members that on them rests a positive duty of working for its growth and expansion. If that is done, and apostolic movements are begun under sound ecclesiastical guidance, there will be little in the way of success that will be denied them. If all are called to the apostolate (and it is certain that they are), each will receive from God the actual graces needed for success in his work. Every kind of objection will be raised against this widespread organization of the laity; many possibilities of harm will be quoted. But an answer always lies to hand in the supernatural helps the Almighty is committed to bestow.

We hear it said time and time again that the lay apostle is certain to commit many indiscretions. And suppose that were true? Does one refuse a harvest because a few ears of corn might be spoiled by clumsy handling? Is the only possible safeguard against such indiscretions a shameful inaction? Rather think in terms of careful discipline, earnest guidance and the grace of God! The history of the lay apostolate to date does not suggest that indiscretions either serious or numerous need be anticipated. Cardinal Newman declares:

"They who are ever taking aim make no hits; they who never venture never gain; to be ever safe is to be ever feeble; to do some substantial good, is the compensation for much incidental imperfection."

XI. A TASK FOR CATHOLIC EDUCATORS

It has been established that conquest ought to be an essential note of Christianity. Catholicism that is not apostolic is lacking in a vital ingredient. Each member of the Church is baptized, "holy-communioned" and confirmed unto the apostolate; each is meant to be a soldier and, as such, each has the inescapable duty of fighting, not only against the temptations which afflict him personally, but against all the mighty forces arrayed against the Mystical Body of Christ in the world to-day.

On the realization of this vital Christian principle the whole future of the world may well depend. Even while these unambitious pages were being compiled, the world situation seriously deteriorated with the result that the sharp delineation between the forces of Christ and of Antichrist has become even more evident. The latter are advancing in every department of life. They have almost captured the centers of intellectual culture; they have successfully infiltrated into the Trade Union and other labor movements; they have established themselves, usually through Satanic trickery, as the political masters of a large proportion of the Old World. Yet, their campaign has only just begun. They will not rest until every adversary is crushed and powerless. At present they often disguise themselves as angels of light; later they will reveal themselves for what they are—the worst enemies of our Christian civilization.

1. Meeting a Subtle Attack

Their attack is being made with scientific subtlety on every front, and is so artfully designed that none, even the most secluded, can escape its impact. They have intoxicated our race with materialism, made it incapable of applying even the first principles of reason to the fact and purpose of human existence. The great scientific advances of the last decades, culminating in the harnessing of atomic power, have been used principally for the removal of whatever can be called pain and for the perfecting of the means of destruction. Integral paganism is the order of the day.

Thinking men realize, just as the powers of darkness realize, that only one force capable of saving civilization is left in our world, and that force is Catholicism. But the tragedy is that for the most part our religion is not being practised as integral Catholicism. It is weak, maimed, lacking in essentials. It is true that Catholics are almost the only remaining large body of regular church-goers; it is true that one can still see crowded altar rails, as the faithful flock to receive their Sacramental Lord; it is true that there are within the Church many flourishing excellent associations. Nevertheless, it cannot be denied that too many of us tend to regard life as being composed of two distinct elements, the secular and the religious. For millions within the Church, life means little more than the carving out of a successful career, plus the enjoyment of the maximum amount of pleasure, plus the saving of one's soul. But, in reality, life is meant to be the outflowering of the divine life of sanctifying grace in and through the right doing of daily tasks as God-given. It is not sufficiently realized that being a Catholic is an absolutely whole-time job, that there is no sphere of human activity which cannot be "catholicized"—or, better, "divinized." Still more, it is not realized that Catholicism carries with it the obligation of being always and everywhere an apostle of Christ.

2. Integral Christianity versus Integral Paganism

At this moment when the forces of evil have well-nigh succeeded in bringing about a world revolution, the Catholic body seems far from convinced that it is called upon to do the same thing. Integral paganism must be confronted with integral Christianity, and that can only come about when the apostolic spirit saturates the whole Church. Perhaps it is an oversimplification to consider cold figures. The complete conversion of the United States of America, for instance, means that some 24 million people must convert about 110 million—that one person must convert at most five others to the Church. That is surely not a great task for a lifetime. Actually, much less would be required because each one of those influenced would also be called upon to influence others, and thus the apostolic effort would be cumulative. Wave would pile upon wave until an irresistible force would sweep forward.

However that may be, it is evident that the sense of conquest, so characteristic of the early Christians in their conflict with Roman paganism, must be restored to the Church in our day. The more pagan the world becomes, the more helpless the clergy are rendered. "What would the Twelve have done," asks Pope Pius XI, "if they had not gathered around them men and women, the old and the young, saying: 'We carry with us the treasure of heaven. Help us to scatter it abroad'?" The world cannot be converted by the clergy alone; the coöperation of the laity is essential. If the Catholic people in any country are not being trained to give that coöperation, if they are being denied the opportunity, if they are being educated to irresponsibility and inaction, if the sense of mission is not present amongst them, if they have no realization of their duty to others, if they are not public-spirited—then the Church in that place is not healthy; it is in peril, and sooner or later the peril will find it out.

It is clear that a vital part in the fostering of the apostolic, militant spirit can and ought to be played by our Catholic educators. Here is a quotation from the *American Ecclesiastical Review* (May, 1945):

"The present educational program, they frankly say, is limited to instilling in the student the belief that his first and practically his only business is to save his own soul. Not much is said about his obligation to sanctify others as he would sanctify himself. The student finishes his course deeply imbued with his responsibility to love God above all things, but little concerned with loving his neighbor as himself, except in terms of giving money or material help to the poor. It seldom even occurs to him that he has within him that truth for which men are yearning, or that many with whom he daily rubs elbows will never in their lifetime partake of that truth if it is not in some small measure communicated to them by himself."

Year after year Catholic teachers—priests, religious and laity throughout the world—launch into the melée of life many thousands of young people. How many of them have been educated in the ideal of the apostleship? How many of them are firmly convinced that they have a duty to make their influence felt, if only in their own particular little circle of acquaintances? How many of them are going to take part in the social life of their environment? Yet, Père Plus can define a Christian as one to whom God has entrusted the care of his fellow-men! Well might one ask regarding the products of our Catholic schools: "Are these the integral Catholics who are being pitted against integral paganism in the world to-day?"

3. Lack of Red-Hot Apostles

Facts prove that our modern Catholic educational system—be it in the home, the school, or the parish —is not producing red-hot apostles. One questions whether the duty of all to be apostles is even being taught in many of our schools. If it is being taught, it is taught in such a way that the pupils do not appreciate its meaning and importance. There is, indeed, much evidence in support of the theory that the children regard religion as just one more subject on the curriculum, in which examinations are to be passed as in the case of algebra or geography. Otherwise, how could it happen that the youth of probably the most loyal Catholic nation under the sun are notorious for the ease with which they forsake their religion when confronted with the materialism of a neighboring land?

Catholic education should be designed towards the instilling of a sense of responsibility into those who are fortunate enough to receive it. Graduates of our schools live amongst their fellows whose immortal souls are in darkness, who are groping for the light and cannot find it, who are seeking happiness in impossible places. Yet, few of these graduates seem to feel any liability towards their less fortunate brethren. They have the key to the happiness of the world; either they are unaware of that fact, or they do not know how to use the key. Could any greater tragedy be imagined? Here is a world full of grave problems of every description. All folk do is to talk airily about them and leave them to this society or that, as if these societies were fairy godmothers divorced from individuals. Ultimately, the curing of evils comes only from the inner urge of individuals. It is the task of Catholic education to instill this sense of responsibility for others. At present too many people have a soft, cowardly, negative attitude towards life; individuals are not playing their part in solving the grave evils that beset society; our Catholic young people, who possess the key to these problems, are failing to face them. The result is that irreligion is growing unchecked. Religious education which results in such a state of affairs can hardly be called successful.

4. Shirking Our Responsibilities

Catholic education is not limited to the training imparted in the school. It goes on throughout life; many agencies take part in it. Yet, it seems that all neglect this essential element in an integral Catholic life—the apostolate or the duty of passing on to others the faith that lives in one's own soul. For example, a priest is entrusted with a parish; to his care are committed the souls, not only of his Catholic people, but also of the non-Catholics who live in the parish. Canon Law tells him that he has a responsibility to the latter. The apostolic priest will regard it as his God-given task to develop to the full the spiritual potentiality of all under his care, to bring the faith to those who have it not and to make of his parish a power-house from which will radiate the warmth and light of the Gospel. All that will be the object of the education of his people, and he will consider himself to have failed precisely in so far as those objectives are not attained. In the pursuit of them he will realize his own inadequacy and welcome the assistance of his people; indeed, one of his first ambitions will be to enlist the help of as many of them as possible in the great work which lies before him. Religious education—whether it be by the priest in the pulpit, the teacher in the school or the parent in the home—is being debased when it is devoted to the turning out of the merely conventional Catholic. In fact, we should cease to use the word Catholic merely as an adjective; it must become life itself.

5. A Practical Solution

How can all this be done? The best answer to that is to describe a parish of our acquaintance in which the priests were united in their effort to attain the Catholic ideal. It is a parish of about a thousand families and four thousand people. Four groups of zealous lay folk were formed with the express purpose of helping the clergy in their work. Each group meets weekly, and each of the meetings is of the same construction. The Prayer to the Holy Ghost and five Mysteries of the Rosary are said, and followed by a short spiritual reading. The minutes of the previous meeting are heard and approved. Reports on apostolic work allocated at the last meeting follow; each member speaks in turn, the others taking part in the discussion of the cases when necessary. The *Magnificat* is said, and the priest then gives a talk directed towards the spiritual or technical formation of the members. Work is allocated for the next week, other business is discussed, and the meeting concludes with prayer and the priest's blessing.

The first work undertaken was a house-to-house

census of the whole parish. Each home, Catholic and non-Catholic, was visited. Very many Catholic families and individuals not on the parochial books were found. At non-Catholic homes an effort was made to interest the occupants in some aspect of the Faith and leaflets were left. The census completed, a campaign was started for membership in the parish confraternities. Men's, women's, boys' and girls' groups all took part and met with very great success. This was followed by a Daily Mass Crusade and a recruiting drive for the Knights, Handmaids and Pages of the Blessed Sacrament, who promise to receive Holy Communion weekly. Needless to say, perhaps, the number of Holy Communions received in the parish has more than quadrupled itself since the beginning of this work.

Now each of these groups is carrying on the apostolate as required by the priest. As many as possible of the weaker brethren of the parish are visited weekly in their homes; days of recollection are organized; the devotion of the Night Adoration is being spread; Catholic literature is distributed; the sick are visited, and so on. Two of the groups consist of teen-agers, one of boys and the other of girls. Between them, with a little assistance from the seniors, they conduct the youth movement in the parish. Efficient clubs for both boys and girls are run, with a limited amount of mixed activity. In these an effort is made to meet every reasonable requirement of the young people themselves.

Non-Catholics are not neglected. Periodically, printed invitations are distributed to their homes for lectures or other events in the parish specially designed to appeal to them. The response is usually gratifying, and many converts have already been received as a result of these activities.

The significance of this work is that, merely by devoting a few hours each week to their training and formation, the clergy of the parish have at their disposal some eighty workers, each of whom does at least two hours' active work every week. The clergy admit that through their sacrifice in directing these four Præsidia of the Legion of Mary a completely new spirit has permeated the parish; priests and people seem united in the twofold work of sanctifying themselves and radiating the Faith around them. Many sensational conversions of different kinds have taken place; attendance at Mass and Benediction has noticeably increased; the parish societies are flourishing.

In this parish it is true to say that between those working actively and those giving the help of their prayers, and those being worked for, the whole population has been taken in, and raised from the level of neglect or routine to that of enthusiastic membership of the Church. That is surely true Catholic education. And the same thing could be done in every place: the whole population could be organized for God; a mighty force could be unleashed which would spread like a contagion from one to another, making the ideals of self-sacrifice, mutual love and idealism pleasing and acceptable to all, causing each to think in terms of service, ending frustration, and offering to all the opportunity to respond to the great call of the Popes for a militant apostolic laity. Integral Catholics are not made merely by exhortation; from their earliest years they must be brought into active contact with the apostolic life of the Church; they must grow up in the atmosphere of the apostolate; they must take the apostolate for granted as normal Catholicism—for that is what it is. Catholicism that is not apostolic is subnormal; and to educate our people to subnormality is, not only to rob them of their rights, but to deprive the world of any chance of that Christian revolution which must take place if the powers of darkness are to be thwarted.

XII. SOCIAL ACTION AND THE CATHOLIC APOSTOLATE

ONE OF THE THINGS most insistent in the writings and speeches of the Popes of recent years has been the appeal to members of the Church to engage in the social apostolate.

"Those many Catholics," wrote Leo XIII in *Rerum Novarum*, "who, because they understand the needs of the times, exert every effort to improve in becoming fashion the lot of the workingman, are most worthy of praise."

In the letter, *Il Fermo Proposito*, Leo's successor urged Catholics "to take the interests of the people supremely to heart, and especially those of the workingman and farm laborer. Do not be content only with instilling the principle of religion—the only source of consolation in the difficulties of life—into the hearts of all; seek to dry their tears, to ease their pains, to improve their economic conditions with wisely-regulated provisos."

1. Work for the Workers

In 1919 Benedict XV exhorted the specialists in Catholic Action "to turn particular attention and care towards the working classes." The late Holy Father, Pius XI, praises all priests and laymen who concern themselves "with special zeal for the social question" (*Quadragesimo Anno*).

Again he declares: "It is of the utmost importance to foster in all classes of society an intensive program of social education. . . . Catholic Action must organize propaganda on a large scale to disseminate knowledge of the fundamental principles on which, according to the Pontifical documents, a Christian Social Order must build" (*Divini Redemptoris*).

The objectives of this Christian Social Apostolate have been outlined by standard writers on the subject as four:

(1) to realize a level of social justice conformable to the principles of the Gospel;
(2) to practise charity by helping people in their material necessities;
(3) to secure the moral uplifting of the people by easing their material difficulties;
(4) to garrison faith and morals in the working-man by showing him that the Church is interested in his material as well as in his spiritual welfare.

It will be seen at once that these aims are much more restricted than those appointed by the Popes for Catholic Action. "The supreme objective towards which all our efforts must converge is the establishment of the human race under the rule of Our Lord, Jesus Christ" (*E Supremi Apostolatus*). "Catholic Action sets before itself the diffusion of Christ's Kingdom among individuals, in the family and throughout society" (Pius XI to the Primate of Spain, November 6, 1929).

"Catholic Action belongs, not to the material, but to the spiritual order; to the heavenly, not the earthly; to the religious, not the political" (*Quæ Nobis*).

2. *Catholic Action's Aim*

Many more passages could be quoted, but they are all adequately summed up by Civardi (*Manual of Catholic Action*, page 240):

"The proper end of Catholic Action is the advent of the reign of Christ—a *religious* end. Social-economic works, on the other hand, have as proper and direct aim the material well-being of their associates—an *economic* aim, however fully it be subordinate to higher aims of a religious and moral order. . . . These higher aims, which for Catholic Action are direct, for social-economic works are only indirect, i.e., are sought and realized by way of other specific aims. . . . The objective of Catholic Action is *universal*—to restore all things in Christ; to assist the Hierarchy in *every* apostolic need. Social-economic works have but a *partial* objective, a program limited to what concerns the welfare of their proper associates and the safeguard of their legitimate interests."

On paper and in theory these differences are perfectly easy to understand. But it is an undeniable fact that in practice Catholic Action has become almost entirely identified with the social apostolate.

3. A New Approach?

It is said—it has even been said in the English Catholic press—that the de-Christianization of the world has progressed too far to permit of any approach being made to the people in the name of Christ, that the idea of going direct to them on a religious mission is quite out of the question, and that a long-drawn-out preliminary process of preparing the soil has to be carried out. This preparatory work must be on the Catholico-economic level—cultural rather than religious.

"How long is this process to take?" one of its advocates was asked recently.

"Four or five generations is usually estimated," came the reply.

"So that during those four or five generations the direct religious approach is to be abandoned?"

"There is no question of abandoning it. We would use it if we believed it would be effective, but we are convinced that it cannot be. Materialism has progressed too far for that. The important thing nowadays is for Catholicism to make itself heard in public life; there must be some counter-blast to Communism. Following the appeal of the Popes, we must Christianize every department of life. That is the aim of our movement."

Now, there can be little doubt that the Catholic social-economic movement will do immense good, but that good will be very much diminished if the movement tries to capture the whole field of Catholic Action for itself by persisting in the contention that the best or only way to approach the masses today is through the social question.

The idea that a direct approach to men in the name of Christ is nowadays impossible, is surely a complete betrayal of the mission of the Church. It is a flat denial of the teaching of Christ Himself and of St. Paul; it is a travesty of the lessons of church history and a thorough misinterpretation of the mind of the great social Encyclicals. "Seek ye therefore first the kingdom of God and His justice: and all these things shall be added unto you" (Matt., vi. 33).

The world into which Christ came was very like our own in many respects. St. Paul's description of the pagan Rome of his day might easily have been penned of the people of our time: "They are versed in every kind of injustice, knavery, impurity, avarice and ill-will; spiteful, murderous, contentious, deceitful, depraved, backbiters, slanderers, God's enemies; insolent, haughty, vain-glorious; inventive in wickedness, disobedient to their parents; without prudence, without honor, without love, without loyalty, without pity." But how did St. Paul convert them? Was it by preaching to them a social-economic program? Was it by approaching them on merely a cultural level? Was it by trying to make them human by way of preparation for the teaching of Christ? Indeed, no!

The very center of Paulinism is Christ. "Everything," says Fernand Prat, "converges on this point; thence everything proceeds, and thither everything returns. Christ is the beginning, middle, and end of everything. In the natural order, as in the supernatural, everything is in Him, everything is by Him, everything is for Him" ("The Theology of St. Paul," II, 13). "So it was, brethren, that when I came to you and preached Christ's message to you, I did so without any high pretensions to eloquence or to philosophy. *I had no thought of bringing you any other knowledge than that of Jesus Christ, and of Him as crucified*" (I Cor., ii. 2).

One wonders if the Romans and the Corinthians, the Ephesians and the Colossians, the Galatians, the Thessalonians and the Philippians would ever have been converted if St. Paul had begun by telling them that he had come amongst them to improve their social and economic conditions, or if he had come to the conclusion that they were too wicked to receive the Gospel of Christ immediately!

4. St. Paul's Greatness

The headline set by St. Paul was, of course, maintained throughout the history of the Church. In fact, one of the greatest lessons of ecclesiastical history is precisely that men were only made to realize fully their humanity through the acceptance of the teaching of Christ. It was by preaching Him that Christianity proved itself to be the source, measure and nursery of all true civilization. It was by preaching Him that it tamed the Germanic hordes during the epoch of the migration of the nations, and out of barbarism evolved order.

It was by preaching Him that Patrick converted Ireland, Augustine England, and Boniface Germany. It was by preaching Him that the Franciscans and the Dominicans in the fourteenth century covered Asia from the Volga to the Desert of Gobi with their missionary stations. It was by preaching Him, too, that the sons of St. Ignatius in later times established themselves as the spearhead of the forward march of Christendom. In short, it was by confronting men with Christ and Him Crucified that Christianity transformed and elevated society, softened and refined it, and established it firmly in law and order.

Would all this work have been achieved, one is tempted to ask, if other methods had been employed —if, for instance, the great Saint-apostles had judged it necessary to prepare peoples for Christ by a long "softening-up" process, consisting in an attempt to apply Christian social principles to a pagan society?

"Yet, surely the whole trend of the great social Encyclicals is that the principal stress should be placed on the social apostolate?" I beg to differ. I would say that the center of all the great Papal pronouncements to-day as at all times has been the same as the center of the teaching of St. Paul—Jesus Christ. "As these evils crowd in upon us," asked the present Pope on Easter Day, 1940, "what hope of remedy is left to us except that which comes from Christ, from His inspirations, and from His teaching, a healing stream flowing through every vein of society? *Only* Christ's law, *only* Christ's grace, can renew and restore private and public life, redressing the true balance of rights and duties, checking unbridled self-interest, controlling passion, implementing and perfecting the course of strict justice with His overflowing charity. He who could once give His commands to wind and storm, who could allay the waves of an angry sea and reduce them to calm, He it is who *alone* can turn men's hearts to peace and brotherly love; He *alone* can bid the nations settle their disputes, freely and successfully, not by violence, but by the law of truth, of justice and charity. . . ." Yes, Christ and Christ *alone!*

5. *Papal Pronouncements on Catholic Action*

A careful study of all Papal utterances and pronouncements of the last sixty years or so will prove that any emphasis on the social apostolate has only been so placed in so far as social betterment is bound to result from the persevering and intense application of the religious system of the Church. It is manifestly impossible to take the principles found in *Rerum Novarum* or *Quadragesimo Anno* and apply them to society as it is to-day. Something else is necessary first—a return to Christ. Listen to Pope Pius XI:

> "This longed-for social reconstruction must be *preceded* by a profound renewal of the Christian spirit, from which multitudes engaged in industry have unhappily departed. *Otherwise, all our efforts will be futile.* . . . 'If society is to be healed now'—We use the words of Our Predecessor—'in no way can it be healed save by a return of Christian life and Christian institutions,' for Christianity *alone* can apply an efficacious remedy for the excessive solicitude for transitory things which is the origin of all vices." (*Quadragesimo Anno*).

One who is anxious to study exactly the mind of the Popes on this exceedingly important matter should not omit to consider the highly significant fact that in the one Encyclical called "The Reconstruction of the Social Order" special emphasis is placed on lay retreats. After mentioning Christian organizations and study groups, the Holy Father continues:

> "But, *above all,* let them hold in high esteem and assiduously employ for the good of their disciples that most valuable means of both personal and social restoration which is to be found in the spiritual exercises."

The purpose of these retreats must be the production not of glib orators to proclaim the application of Christian social principles, but of

> "true apostles . . . enkindled with the fire of the *Heart of Christ* . . . strong in faith, endowed with invincible steadfastness in persecution, burning with zeal, *interested solely in spreading everywhere the Kingdom of Christ.*"

6. *Record Low Level of Spiritual Literature*

Recent years have witnessed a vast output of literature, an enormous stream of oratory, and a regular spate of so-called Catholic Action movements, operating mostly on the level of sociology and economics. At the same time there has everywhere been an increasingly marked reluctance to speak openly of religious matters, to approach men directly in the name of Christ.

The output of solid spiritual literature has reached a record low level; pious associations and confraternities are not receiving anything like the support and encouragement of former days. Long-established and beneficial devotional practices are lapsing through disuse. In England the attendance at evening service is gradually diminishing; in many places Sunday School has gone altogether, and there is a universal craving for short and "snappy" services. All these are further indications—and there are others—of the general trend of Catholic life. Superfluous surely to add that the trend is all in the wrong direction.

The lines which have been written lead inexorably to certain conclusions. Firstly, if the repeated call of the Popes to all to engage in the apostolate is to become effective and yield results, it is absolutely imperative that the difference between real, authentic Catholic Action and Social Action be emphasized again and again. It is a great evil that the whole field should be occupied by work which, good though it may be, is largely on the natural level, and that a genuine spiritual apostolate, the transmission of the Christ-life from soul to soul, should in practice be excluded. For the latter alone is essentially Catholic Action, the sharing by the laity in the priestly work of the salvation and sanctification of souls.

Secondly, it must be universally understood that,

before Catholic social principles can be applied to society, a return to Christ is necessary; therefore, the most vital and most important thing is a *spiritual* apostolate, the direct presentation of Christ to men.

Thirdly, there is no truth whatever in the contention that the last-mentioned work is impossible. The spiritual apostolate has been possible for nearly twenty centuries of Catholicism, and it is just as possible to-day as ever it has been.

Fourthly, the slogan, "Humaniser avant de Christianiser," represents a false principle and should have no part whatever in Catholic life.

Fifthly, the *greatest* necessity of the day is not knowledge, either of apologetics or social principles, but holiness, the only true source of an effective apostolate. It is false to say that a "sacristified" youth (i.e., one who has been most in contact with the altar) is less likely to succeed as an apostle than one who, because he is barely practising his religion, is said to be more attuned to the pagan milieu in which he lives.

7. *A Challenge to Paganism*

The following lines appeared a few months ago in an English Catholic magazine:

"We are living in a pagan country. Those about us are perfectly ignorant of religious fundamentals and completely apathetic towards anything connected with the Church. Why should our approach to them be mainly on the social justice level? Could we not adopt rather the technique of the missionaries working in the African jungles, i.e., concentrate on the effective presentation of Catholicism in all its beauty?"

Shortly afterwards came this reply: "As for the opinion that we adopt the technique of missionaries, such would only lead to ridicule, as the average man to-day is immediately suspicious of any attempt to lead him to a Church." What then? Must the apostolate be suspended or must it be relegated to the merely natural level, as we have so severely deprecated above? Neither; it must go on. Just as in the time of St. Paul, those must be found to-day who will rejoice to be fools for Christ's sake, to hunger and thirst, to be naked and buffeted and homeless, to be reviled, persecuted and blasphemed, to become the very refuse of the world that the name of Christ might be preached (cfr. I Corinthians, iv. 9-13, 14).

Is that mere rhetoric, representing a dream impossible of attainment? The most practical answer to such a question is surely the Legion of Mary. Here is a movement which expressly and of set purpose concentrates on the waging of a spiritual apostolate "to enlighten those who are in darkness and in the shadow of death, to inflame those who are lukewarm, to bring back to life those who are dead in sin," and it is probably the most successful lay movement in the Church to-day.

Veritable miracles have been wrought by its members in every stratum of society in every quarter of the globe. No one who is sincere and animated by zeal for souls can afford to ignore such a movement. There are many who are convinced that it holds a key position to-day in world Catholic Action. The Apostolic Delegate to Missionary Africa has said that he considered the movement to be the nearest approach yet made to the ideal of Catholic Action as fostered by the Holy Father:

> "Catholic Action decked out in attractive and alluring form; throbbing with life so that it wins all to it; undertaken in the manner stipulated by Pius XI, that is, in dependence on the Virgin Mother of God; insistent on quality as the foundation of membership and even as the key to numerical strength; safeguarded by plenteous prayer and self-sacrifice, by exact system, and by complete coöperation with the priest."

8. Needed Prayer plus Action

It needs only a little experience of the Legion of Mary to realize that it is no mere praying organization, no mere pious association, but one of intense action—undertaking work that is infinitely more difficult, unpleasant and daring than is done by any branch of Catholic Action in the world. It provides for the carrying on of the traditional Catholic apostolate. If the soil is favorable, it will exploit it; if the soil is unfavorable, it will nevertheless not desist from working it.

It ensures the preaching of Christ and the bringing of religion into every pursuit of life. It offers the priest a standard system for the spiritual, psychological and practical training of the lay apostles whom the Popes have bidden him gather around him to assist him in his apostolate, and it is now a matter of solid worldwide experience that Legion spirituality and the Legion method of the apostolate have combined to make a movement that has not only found approval with every ecclesiastical authority from highest to lowest, and proved to have a unique power of attracting the laity to itself, but a movement which by its amazing spread throughout the world and its astonishing harvest of souls has proved that it is indeed especially blessed of heaven.

9. Fallacy of Sociological Christianity

Since the above was written, an editorial on the same subject has appeared in the English Dominican periodical, *Blackfriars* (September, 1947). With the permission of the Editor, we print the following extracts as being useful in emphasizing an important subject from a slightly different point of view.

"The need for insisting quite simply on the one and only End of all activity remains the most urgent. The bookstalls are packed with books and journals dealing, in truth or speciously, with the detailed problems of society. There are now even many Catholic reviews and magazines which compete in the fields of politics, economics and culture with the general periodical literature coming from the thousands of pagan pens writing with Christian ink. . . .

"But the danger of losing sight of the wood on account of the great number and proximity of the trees is all the greater, the more specialized and detailed the treatment becomes. The main subject is human life in its various aspects and activities, and, in so far as this concerns movements towards one or many ends, it can only be seen in proportion, and even in reality, in relation to the end. The movement and the action receive their character, their form, from the goal at which they are aiming. And in human life that goal must be God objectively, and the happiness of the beatific vision subjectively. Human life and human action are ultimately good or bad in relation to this end, and so it depends on that end whether they are truly human, truly social, truly cultural. The true wholeness of human nature and human life can only be realized in terms of the vision of God. Man is split in a hundred pieces by all these detailed analyses of modern problems; and he can only be put together again by referring them all to the higher supernatural reality of the Trinity and our share in the life of the Trinity. That is where integration must ultimately be sought. . . . But the danger of calling oneself a champion of human integrity is that human integrity itself becomes the end of man instead of the effect of man's having achieved that end. In other words, if we set out to solve our acute human problems precisely in order to become more human, to acquire more perfection for our natures in the arts as well as in religion, in society as well as in our private hobbies, then God Himself and the vision of Him become a means, the balance of creation is lost, and the whole structure comes toppling down. . . .

"Apart from Catholicism, Christianity has lost its grip of dogma and the true, unsullied teaching about the nature of God and His perfections and operations. And because in this way the end of human life has become vague and uninteresting, the various religions have declined into a post-Christian state in which the be-all and end-all of human endeavor have become the physical happiness of man on this earth, the development of his faculties, and the avoidance of the pains which come his way. In other words, the test of the modern Christian is whether he is a well-developed specimen of the human race and whether he is assisting others to become so. In this way sociology— significantly a new science—has become a characteristic preoccupation of the Christian. He is only a true Christian if he has done something to better the lot of the working classes and has interested himself in social clubs and worker movements.

The love of God in Himself and His worship no longer specify the Christian life; it is the service of man for man which has taken the place of the divine aims which the Church sets before us.

"Sociological Christianity is the best that religion seems to be able to offer in these days. And to bring grace violently into the picture is to use God and His gifts for economic and cultural aims. It is the self-conscious expression of religion seeking to justify itself in the eyes of the world. For 'the world' to-day can only recognize as good that which brings individual men material benefits—that is, benefits which give comfort and ease to the man, be it tobacco, Tolstoi, or travel. It does seek to justify and propagate a human attitude to work, but even so this type of social thought has been occasioned outside Christianity by the pagan forces of rationalism and materialism.

"There is, in fact, some truth in the opponents to Christianity who say that there would be none of this insistence on justice to the workers, and the right of each to a fully human existence, had not the non-Christian revolutionaries started the fashion. The Church left to herself seems inclined to overlook these things, or at least she does not organize vast schemes for humanizing the masses, which are so often left 'in the mass' to live a rather dirty and drudged existence.

"Now, the answers which the specialists in these (social) fields are giving are, as we have said, good and necessary. The answers to the problems of work, of inequality of wealth and possessions, of human freedom and culture among the crowd, all these must be tackled by the specialist on the spot in their own spheres. But the Catholic Church *as such* must beware of identifying the teaching of the Church with the solutions offered. The Kingdom of Heaven is not of this world, and until we seek *first* and *completely* the Kingdom of Heaven, these other benefits will not be added unto us. The Catholic, too, is apt to take his standards from the Christians and pagans around him, and to forget the heinous crime of sin in his desire to give more bread and butter to the miner. He is inclined to judge the progress of Catholic life by the number of social clubs and youth organizations. He instinctively begins to regard Christianity from this declared form of it, in which the supreme end has at least partially been lost to view.

"Inevitably when the Catholic adopts standards lower than those he professes every Sunday in the *Confiteor* as well as in the Creed, he falls short of the results of those whose lower standard is the highest they know. There has been a constant insistence upon the social teaching of the Church for many years, and the Catholic worker movements have not only themselves received encouragement from every level of the Church's ecclesiastical life, but have spread widely throughout the world. They have achieved great successes in every place. It was generally regarded as the effect of *Jocist* movements that the first French crisis after the war was met by the M.R.P.; and there are millions of occasions in which the young Catholic worker has bettered the lot of his class through such institutions. No one could deny these benefits nor the good—yes, the *apostolic* good in winning souls to Christ—which these movements have performed. Yet, there are parallels in other Christian communities, and when such non-Christian movements as Communism or Fascism really set their hand to this kind of thing, they seem to achieve even more dramatic results.

"There is one test as to whether the Christian apostolate of the worker is too much caught up in the modern sociological Christianity, a test as to the truly Christian idea of vocation in work. . . . The Catholic Church recently in the Pope's Encyclicals has made it abundantly clear; but we should reflect also that since the earliest ages the Church without any high-flown phrases has always set before men the truly Christian vocation of work in the ranks of her Religious Orders. In those Orders the lay Brothers and lay Sisters have always played an essential and powerful part. And only in those ranks will the Christian find a complete outline of holy work which is saintly in emptying slops, saintly in scrubbing floors, with the same sanctity as the 'work' of the subdeacon in placing the chalice upon the altar.

"Now, it is in this very point that the Catholic social apostolate fails. Despite the vast worker movements, or perhaps because of them, the number of lay Brothers and lay Sisters has declined rapidly. Some Orders to-day have even abandoned the idea of having them, and have had to reorganize the whole structure of their Religious life. The number and fervor of these members of Religious Orders, men and women who reach the heights of sanctity more simply and more frequently than their more sophisticated 'choir' brethren and sisters, should be the thermometer of the healthiness of our social teaching.

"So far this teaching has tended to be lost in the means, so that the end has disappeared. It becomes 'this-worldly' and man-centered with the rest of present-day Christianity. The final end which is revealed to us through the Cross will alone *sanctify* labor, and it is that which Christ has commissioned His apostles to preach. If the Kingdom of God is honestly sought first, then the social conditions and international problems will tend to be resolved. They obviously can never be wholly resolved because of the continued presence of sin. But until we seek the one and only remedy for sin, namely, the grace of God which is the share in the intimate life of the Blessed Trinity, there can be no improvement at all. Along this way lies integrity. Any other way leads to dissipation.

"St. Thomas, when he was faced with any problem, solved it finally at the foot of the crucifix; and when he came to die, he came to see his vast and superhuman synthesis of truth—worked out in such intricate and coherent detail—all of it as mere straw. He did not deny its truth or validity, but he saw it in perspective. This was not naïvety but wisdom. This was Christian life moving towards its Life."

XIII. TRUE DEVOTION TO MARY
A NECESSARY INGREDIENT

Several years ago I read the works of St. Grignion de Montfort for the first time. I thought they were farfetched and full of pious exaggerations. A holy priest told me to wait, for Our Lady would show me everything. As time went on, I began to understand something of Mary's position in the scheme of salvation as designed by God; I saw the first Eve and the second Eve as the counterparts of the first Adam and the Second. I understood that, as a woman had been instrumental in effecting our condemnation, so God willed that a Woman should play a vital part in our reconciliation. In the Annunciation I saw the reversal of the act of disobedience of the first woman, and I began to feel at last that Mary's consent to the announcing Angel was an act of the highest importance in the drama of the Redemption. That consent was completed and ratified when she stood at the foot of the Cross offering her Son for the sins of men, redeeming the world with Christ, and by her sorrows bringing forth children of grace. Forever in heaven that work was to continue, and Mary, under the Providence of God, became the Mediatrix of all

Graces. I understood, too, that Catholic Action is simply the continuation among men of the work of Redemption, and that the best possible model for it would be that established by the all-seeing Providence of God Himself.

Pius XI defined Catholic Action as the participation by the laity in the apostolate of the Church's Hierarchy. Therefore, the aim, end, or object of Catholic Action must be the same as that of the Hierarchy itself—the establishing of the whole human race under the kingship of Our Lord, Jesus Christ. *"Instaurare omnia in Christo,"* said Pius X, "has always been the motto of the Church." That is the supreme aim of Catholic Action—to establish the Kingdom of Christ, to lead souls to God. In other words, it is a continuation of the work of the Redemption, a perpetuation of the Incarnation. Now, whether we advert to it or not, every grace of Catholic Action is bestowed through Mary; every soul that is led to God, is led by Mary; no new stronghold of the Kingdom of Christ that is established, is established without the active coöperation of Mary. Just as Mary, by the will of God, took such an intimate, such a vital, part in the work of our Redemption, so does she still by her universal mediation take an essential part in the continuation of that work by the Mystical Body of Christ. All the work of the Hierarchy is accomplished with the help of graces bestowed through Mary; and Catholic Action, the sharing by the laity in that work of the Hierarchy, is also made fruitful by means of graces bestowed through Mary. Therefore, why not make explicit in the organization of the lay apostolate the recognition of the overwhelming influence of the Mediatrix of all Graces, the Mother of God?

Regarding the matter from a slightly different angle, the lay apostolate is the collaboration of the laity in the continuation by the Hierarchy of the work of Christ's Eternal Priesthood. We understand, of course, that Christ alone is substantially priest—priest by nature. Of Him, and of Him alone, was it written: "Thou art a priest forever according to the order of Melchisedech." Now, if Christ is priest by nature, it follows that His ordination took place at the very moment at which He became Man. As God only, He could not be priest, for a priest is a mediator between God and man. As the Angelic Doctor put it: "Christ is not priest as God but as man; yet, it is the same Person who is God and priest." Now, if Our Lord became priest at the very moment of His Incarnation, it follows that His ordination took place within the most pure womb of Mary. What temple could be more fitting? No shadow of wickedness had ever crossed its threshold; nothing unbecoming could be found within its walls. Its sacred Custodian was the Spirit of God; He had adorned that sanctuary with flowers of the sublimest virtues; He had protected it from the slightest defilement. The consent of Mary was the sign for the sacred ceremony to begin, and, with attendant angels around, the Divine Anointing of the Hypostatic Union took place, the uncreated Chrism of the Divinity was poured forth from heaven. From an altar of ordination, Mary became an altar of sacrifice, for from the very first moment of His human existence Christ, living in Mary, offered Himself for the restoration of the divine life of men. She it was, indeed, who prepared the Divine Victim for the eternal sacrifice of Calvary. Therefore, by the Providence of God, Mary is inseparably connected with the priesthood of Christ.

1. Mary the Link between Laity and Priesthood

But the laity also are inseparably connected with the priesthood of Christ: being His members, redeemed by Him, they are in all things made like to Him, even to sharing in His priesthood and mission. True, by the Sacrament of Orders certain men are consecrated to the priesthood properly so-called, and act officially in the name of Christ on behalf of the Church. But an analogous participation in Christ's priesthood is conferred by the sacramental character of Baptism and more fully by Confirmation, common to all the faithful, and shared by them in proportion as they identify themselves with Him in the work of Redemption, by their expiatory and meritorious works. For the whole generation of Christians, rightly called by the Prince of the Apostles "a chosen generation, a kingly priesthood, must offer sacrifice for sins, both for themselves and for the whole human race" (Pius XI, *Miserentissimus*). They have, too, in the call to Catholic Action a share in the Apostolic Mission.

Now, as the priesthood of Christ Himself was so intimately connected with Mary, so must every participation in that priesthood be connected with her. Catholic Action, the working in the Mystical Body of the Apostolic Mission, is dependent upon Mary. Every grace it needs, every good it accomplishes, every progress it makes—all these are bestowed through Mary. That is a fact. That is the scheme of things willed by God. Then again, why not give actual and practical expression to that fact in the working out of Catholic Action? Why not vow its collective and individual dependence upon Mary? Seeing how God willed to begin in Mary and through Mary and with Mary, so should the lay apostolate continue the work of the priesthood of Christ amongst men.

Every lay apostle must regard his or her personal sanctification as a primary obligation. That sanctification is only accomplished dependently upon Mary, whether the apostle is conscious of it or not. Such is the will of God. Therefore, the logical thing to do is for each apostle to make explicit acknowledgement of his dependence upon Mary in the task of sanctifying himself. Thankfully will he acknowledge that, not only was the physical Body of Christ formed in Mary's womb, but that there was also formed there a spiritual body, consisting of all those who were to believe in Him. Mary, he knows, bore within her womb, not Christ only, but also those whose life was contained in the life of the Saviour. St. Augustine appreciated that fact long ago when he wrote:

> "All the predestinate, in order to be conformed to the image of the Son of God, are in this world hidden in the womb of the most holy Virgin, where they are protected, nourished, brought up and made to grow by that good Mother, until she has brought them forth to glory after death, which is properly the day of their birth, as the Church calls the death of the just."

There is the image which must be constantly impressed upon every apostle—the image of a life utterly, totally, entirely and absolutely dependent upon our Mother. No other image is adequate—not the image of the heart supplying the stream of life-blood to the body, not the image of holy slavery itself, for none can express such complete dependence as the Augustinian image of the unborn babe. That is simply the logical conclusion to be drawn from any appreciation of Mary's relation to the Mystical Body of Christ. Of necessity, piety centered in Christ leads to a deep veneration of and total consecration to the Blessed Virgin, but that veneration, and that consecration, have only the one goal—Christ, the formation of the Christ-life by Mary in each of His members.

2. Mary Forms Us into the Image of Christ

From all that has been said it follows that to veneration of Mary and consecration to her must be joined a loving imitation of her. She it was who gave to the God-made-Man physical form, and in return she was imbued with His spiritual perfection. Most perfectly she transformed herself into His image. Through her faith she was granted the grace of Divine Motherhood; her virginity made her worthy for the operation of the Holy Ghost; her humility, her obedience to the will of God, her perfect love for Him and for all mankind, led her through all the darkness and desolation of the Seven Dolors to the glorious happiness of the first Easter Morn. Her inner life, as she pondered within her heart all the words and deeds of her Divine Child, drew her ever farther into the depths of His Spirit and imprinted upon her the most perfect representation of the spiritual features of Christ. And therefore we strive

humbly to imitate her, soliciting her motherly help
and intercession. Again and again, sick and wounded,
we will return to her, begging of her to tend our
spiritual wounds as once she lavished loving care
upon the wounds of the Body that was handed her
from the Cross. Again and again we will beg of her
to shelter us within her motherly heart, never to let
us go until Christ has been formed perfectly within
us.

Having understood how vital is the work of his
own sanctification through Mary, the sincere apostle
will easily see how necessary it is for the success of
his apostolate. The secret of all success with others,
as we have insisted throughout these pages, lies in
the establishment of personal contact—a fact proved
by the experience of the Church from the time of the
Apostles until the present. But all success also comes
through Mary; every grace of conversion is dis-
pensed by her to whom she wills, when she wills, and
as she wills. Therefore, does it not seem most certain that the instrument fittest for the apostolate of
contact will be the instrument who has deliberately
allowed himself to be formed and spiritually nour-
ished by Mary? Contact with such a soul will be contact with Mary herself. But if this work is to be
effective, there must be a total and unstinted offering
of himself on the part of every apostle. Just as Mary
surrendered herself wholly to the Divine Will for

the accomplishment of the redemption of men, just as she endured agonies indescribable that her motherly office might be perfected, so must every apostle be prepared to give a service that is absolute and unstinted according to the circumstances of his position in life. For the perfection of his own interior life no sacrifice must be too hard; in his apostolic work no task must be too great, no barrier insuperable, no conquest impossible. No service less than the highest, no consecration less than the fullest, no sacrifice less than the bitterest, is in keeping with the high dignity of the lay apostolate. Only in so far as every single member seriously endeavors to model himself upon Mary both in his interior and in his apostolic life, will the ideal of Catholic Action be truly attained. For the ideal of Catholic Action is surely that it may reflect the spirit of Mary herself.